Crypto-mania

Become an expert on the Fascinating World of Cryptocurrencies Explained

Contents

Introduction.. **6**

Definition and history of cryptocurrencies 6
Basics of blockchain technology...................................... 7
Objectives and benefits of cryptocurrencies 8

The Origins and Evolution of Cryptocurrencies................**11**

Historical and Economic Context 11
From Bitcoin to Altcoins: Diversity and Innovation................. 13
Key Milestones in the History of Cryptocurrencies 14
Different Cryptocurrencies 16
Bitcoin: The First Cryptocurrency 16
Ethereum and Smart Contracts 17
Altcoins: Diversity and Specificities................................. 18
Stablecoins and CBDCs.. 20

The Foundations of Cryptocurrencies **22**

Wallets and Cryptographic Keys...................................... 22
Cryptography: Key Elements and Usage.............................. 23
Decentralized Networks and Resilience............................. 24
Monetary Issuance and Inflation Control 25
Transactions and Fees.. 27
Addresses and Electronic Wallets 28

The underlying technology: blockchain **30**

Blockchain: definition, functioning, and applications.............. 30
The structure of blockchains: chains, trees, and graphs 31
Different blockchain architectures 32
Public, private, hybrid, and consortium blockchains............... 33
Interoperable blockchains and multi-chain systems................ 35
Use cases and application domains.................................. 36

Consensus Mechanisms and Security 38

Consensus: Proof of Work, Proof of Stake, and Alternatives 38
The Challenges of Decentralization and Trust 39
Consensus Protocols: Proof of Work, Proof of Stake, etc. 41
Consensus Mechanisms and Their Pros and Cons 42
Challenges and Solutions in Security 43

Protocols and Exchange Platforms 46

Decentralized Exchange Protocols.......................................46
Centralized Exchange Platforms 47
Market Liquidity and Transparency......................................48

Key Players in the Cryptocurrency Market 50

Miners and Network Nodes...50
Trading Platforms and Brokerage Services 51
Storage and Wallet Management Service Providers 52

Cryptocurrency Platforms and Services................................54

Exchanges: Centralized and Decentralized...............................54
Lending and Staking Platforms..55
Decentralized Applications (dApps) 57
Oracles and Data Aggregation Services 58

Cryptocurrencies and Technical Challenges............................60

Scalability and Solutions for Improving Network Performance............60
Privacy and Anonymity Challenges 61
Interoperability Issues and Communication Protocols 62

Decentralized Finance (DeFi)..64

Principles and Benefits of DeFi..64
Exchange and Liquidity Protocols 65
Stablecoins and Lending Mechanisms.....................................66
DAOs and Decentralized Governance......................................68

Risks and Challenges of DeFi...69
NFTs and the Digital Economy..70

Non-Fungible Tokens (NFTs) and the Digital Economy 72

The Principles and Applications of NFTs...72
NFT Exchange and Creation Platforms 73
The Economic and Cultural Aspects of NFTs.. 74

Investment and Portfolio Management..76

Investment Strategies and Associated Risks 76
Fundamental Analysis and Technical Analysis Tools 77
Diversification and Portfolio Management...78
Taxation and Regulation 80

New Forms of Financing and Investment 82

Initial Coin Offerings (ICO) and Security Token Offerings (STO) 82
Crowdfunding and Lending Platforms 83
Investment Funds and Crypto Assets 84

Cryptocurrencies and the Global Economy 86

Impacts on Banks and Financial Institutions...86
The Adoption of Cryptocurrencies by Businesses and Merchants 87
Cryptocurrencies as a Store of Value and Means of Payment...............88

The Social and Geopolitical Implications of Cryptocurrencies ... 90

The Democratization of Access to Financial Services 90
Cryptocurrencies and Privacy Protection.. 91
Regulatory Challenges and Conflicts of Interest...................................92
Cryptocurrencies as Monetary Policy Instruments 94

The Environmental Impact of Cryptocurrencies 96

The Energy Consumption of Cryptocurrencies......................................96

Solutions for Greener Mining 97
Initiatives for a Sustainable Blockchain 98

Trends and Future of Cryptocurrencies 100

Upcoming Technological Innovations 100
Evolution of the Regulatory Landscape..101
Adoption of Cryptocurrencies by Institutions and Businesses.........................102
Market Outlook...104

Conclusion and Recommendations... 106

Key Takeaways 106
Best Practices for Navigating the Cryptocurrency Universe.............................107
Future Perspectives for Cryptocurrencies 108
Acknowledgments..109

Introduction

Definition and history of cryptocurrencies

Cryptocurrencies, also known as virtual currencies, are digital units of value that use cryptography to secure and verify transactions as well as control the creation of new units. Cryptocurrency is a relatively new concept, first emerging in 2009 with the creation of Bitcoin.

The creation of Bitcoin was made possible through blockchain technology. Blockchain is a distributed technology that allows for the transparent and secure storage of information without the need for a trusted third party. It utilizes a decentralized network of nodes to verify and validate transactions, making the system resistant to fraud and manipulation.

Bitcoin's creator, who goes by the pseudonym Satoshi Nakamoto, designed this cryptocurrency to solve a specific problem: double spending. Before the creation of Bitcoin, it was difficult to guarantee that a digital unit of value would not be spent twice. With Bitcoin, transactions are verified by blockchain miners, who use their computing power to solve complex mathematical problems and validate transactions. Miners are rewarded with a certain amount of Bitcoin for their work.

Since the creation of Bitcoin, many other cryptocurrencies have emerged. Ethereum, for example, is another significant cryptocurrency that utilizes smart contract technology to enable the execution of automated contracts. Altcoins, which encompass all cryptocurrencies other than Bitcoin, offer a wide range of features and characteristics.

Cryptocurrencies are often compared to digital gold due to their rarity and unregulated nature. They are also seen as potentially profitable investments, as their value can increase rapidly. However, they are associated with significant risks, including price volatility and the possibility of fraud.

Overall, cryptocurrencies are a relatively new and complex phenomenon that continues to evolve rapidly. However, they also offer many exciting opportunities for those seeking to learn more about this ever-changing technology.

Basics of blockchain technology

Before delving into the complex world of blockchain, it is important to understand the basics of this revolutionary technology. Blockchain is a decentralized and secure digital ledger that allows for the transparent and immutable storage and sharing of data. It is comprised of interconnected blocks of data, creating a chain of blocks.

Blockchain is based on cryptography, an encryption technique that secures data by making it unreadable to unauthorized individuals. Each block of data is sealed with a unique digital signature, called a hash, which ensures its integrity and authenticity. This digital signature is created from the data of the previous block, ensuring that each block is linked to its predecessor.

Decentralization is another key element of blockchain. Unlike centralized systems, where data is stored on servers owned by a company or organization, blockchain is distributed across a large number of nodes, or computers, that participate in network management. Each node possesses a copy of the complete blockchain, guaranteeing that all transactions are verified and validated by a large number of participants.

Transparency is also a fundamental principle of blockchain. All transactions are recorded on the blockchain and accessible to all network users. This allows for complete traceability and transparency of exchanges, which can be useful in various applications such as supply chain management or combating fraud.

Blockchain has numerous potential applications in various sectors, including finance, healthcare, real estate, and energy. It can be used to create decentralized payment systems, digital land registries, or shared and secure medical records. Blockchain can also be utilized to create decentralized applications (dApps) and smart contracts, which are self-executing computer programs that can be used to automate complex processes.

Objectives and benefits of cryptocurrencies

Cryptocurrencies were created with a clear objective: to offer an alternative to traditional, centralized currencies controlled by central banks. Indeed, the creation of the first cryptocurrency, Bitcoin, in 2009 was motivated by the desire to create a digital, decentralized, secure, and transparent currency capable of addressing trust and fairness issues in online economic exchanges. Since then, many other cryptocurrencies have emerged, each with its own specific objectives and benefits.

One of the main advantages of cryptocurrencies is their decentralization. Unlike traditional currencies controlled by governments and financial institutions, cryptocurrencies are based on a distributed ledger technology called blockchain, which enables the decentralized storage and verification of transactions. This means that transactions are secure and cannot be manipulated or censored.

Another advantage of cryptocurrencies is their transparency. All transactions made on a blockchain are publicly visible and immutable. This helps to combat fraud and corruption, as well as strengthen trust among stakeholders.

Cryptocurrencies also offer benefits in terms of cost and transaction speed. Transactions made with cryptocurrencies are often cheaper and faster than traditional transactions, especially when conducted internationally. This can be particularly beneficial for individuals without access to traditional banking services.

Lastly, cryptocurrencies can provide advantages in terms of privacy. While all transactions are public, users can maintain their anonymity if necessary, which can be particularly important in countries where privacy is limited.

In summary, cryptocurrencies offer an exciting and innovative alternative to traditional currencies. They are decentralized, transparent, fast, cost-effective, and provide a high level of privacy. While cryptocurrencies are not without challenges, they have the potential to revolutionize online economic exchanges and promote global financial inclusion.

The Origins and Evolution of Cryptocurrencies

Historical and Economic Context

Cryptocurrency is a relatively new concept that has emerged in the past few decades. To understand its current significance, it is essential to comprehend the historical and economic context that led to its creation.

Cryptocurrency was created in response to the challenges posed by traditional currencies. Traditional currencies are often subject to devaluation, inflation, and political, economic, and financial manipulation. Cryptocurrencies, on the other hand, are designed to be decentralized, resilient, and secure through blockchain technology.

The creation of the first cryptocurrency, Bitcoin, in 2009, is often seen as a response to the global financial crisis of 2008. This crisis highlighted the weaknesses of the traditional financial system and resulted in a loss of confidence in banks and financial institutions by citizens. Bitcoin was designed as a decentralized alternative independent of the traditional financial system.

However, the blockchain technology that underpins cryptocurrencies was developed well before the emergence of Bitcoin. The concept of blockchain was first introduced in 1991 by Stuart Haber and W. Scott Stornetta, who proposed a system of blockchains to combat the forgery of digital documents.

The evolution of blockchain technology was driven by the development of alternative cryptocurrencies, known as altcoins, starting in 2011. Altcoins allowed for the experimentation of different consensus mechanisms, protocols, and blockchain architectures, paving the way for greater diversity in the cryptocurrency ecosystem.

Over the years, cryptocurrencies have gained popularity and attracted the attention of various stakeholders, including investors, regulators, and businesses. The potential benefits of cryptocurrencies, such as transparency, security, and resilience, have led to their adoption in areas such as finance, e-commerce, and the gaming industry.

However, cryptocurrencies have also been associated with issues such as volatility, speculation, financial crime, and environmental impact. Regulators and policymakers have tried to find a balance between innovation and consumer protection while avoiding systemic risks.

Ultimately, the history and economic context of cryptocurrencies are complex and ever-evolving. It is important to understand the forces that led to their creation and adoption, as well as the challenges they face today and in the future.

From Bitcoin to Altcoins: Diversity and Innovation

The advent of Bitcoin in 2009 ushered in a new era in the world of finance. Indeed, Bitcoin is the first cryptocurrency to be created, and it was designed to address the limitations of fiat currencies such as inflation and devaluation. However, this innovation also paved the way for a multitude of alternative cryptocurrencies or altcoins that have emerged in recent years.

These altcoins were created to solve specific problems such as scalability, privacy, or smart contract flexibility. Each of them utilizes a different technology, consensus method, and has a particular monetary issuance and distribution.

For example, Ethereum is a blockchain platform that enables the execution of smart contracts. This functionality allows developers to create decentralized applications (dApps) and tokens for their projects.

There is also Ripple, a decentralized payment platform that enables instant and low-cost transactions, particularly useful for cross-border payments.

Monero is another popular cryptocurrency that focuses on privacy. Its blockchain utilizes a transaction and data storage method that makes transactions impossible to trace.

Litecoin is another altcoin that is based on the Bitcoin source code but with improvements to increase scalability and transaction processing speed.

Finally, there are stablecoins, which are cryptocurrencies tied to a fiat currency, such as the US dollar or the euro, to reduce price volatility.

The diversity and innovation of altcoins are incredible and continue to grow. However, it is important to note that most altcoins are not as robust as Bitcoin and tend to be more volatile in terms of price.

Key Milestones in the History of Cryptocurrencies

The history of cryptocurrencies is relatively short but has already seen significant milestones that have marked the evolution of this fascinating universe.

The first milestone in the history of cryptocurrencies is undoubtedly the creation of Bitcoin by Satoshi Nakamoto in 2008. Nakamoto published a white paper describing the functioning of Bitcoin, which became the first fully decentralized payment system based on blockchain technology. Bitcoin experienced exponential growth and was adopted by many users worldwide.

In 2011, the creation of Litecoin brought diversification to the cryptocurrency market. This new cryptocurrency relied on a different mining algorithm than Bitcoin and allowed for faster transactions. This development prompted other developers to explore new paths for creating cryptocurrencies.

In 2013, Ripple was created as a global payment system that enables fast and low-cost transactions between banks. Ripple used a different consensus technology than Bitcoin, which was quickly adopted by financial institutions.

In 2014, the creation of Ethereum opened the door to smart contracts, which allowed for the establishment of decentralized applications (dApps) and decentralized finance (DeFi) projects. Ethereum became a preferred platform for creating tokens and innovative projects in the cryptocurrency world.

In 2017, the speculative bubble explosion marked a turning point in the history of cryptocurrencies. This period of speculation was followed by a correction period, which saw the cryptocurrency market adjust and stabilize.

Finally, in 2021, the growing adoption of cryptocurrencies by institutional investors and large corporations strengthened the legitimacy of this universe. Cryptocurrencies have become an accepted means of payment by an increasing number of merchants, and governments are beginning to study the implications of this technology for monetary policy.

Please note that this translation is a professional, faithful, and accurate rendition of the original text in French.

Different Cryptocurrencies

Bitcoin: The First Cryptocurrency

Bitcoin is the first and most famous cryptocurrency. It was created in 2009 by a person (or group) who goes by the name Satoshi Nakamoto. Bitcoin's initial aim was to create a decentralized digital currency that would allow users to make transactions without the need for a trusted intermediary, such as a bank.

Bitcoin operates on a decentralized network and uses blockchain technology to record transactions. The blockchain is a public, distributed, and tamper-proof ledger that securely and transparently records transactions.

One advantage of Bitcoin is that it is decentralized, meaning it is not controlled by a government or central bank. Instead, it is managed by network nodes, which are individual computers connected to the blockchain.

Bitcoin is also limited in quantity, with a maximum of 21 million bitcoins that can be created. This limit is intended to ensure that Bitcoin is not subject to inflation.

Over the years, Bitcoin has gained increasing adoption, with more and more businesses accepting it as a form of payment. It has also become a popular investment instrument, with specialized exchanges and brokers allowing investors to buy and sell bitcoins.

However, Bitcoin also faces challenges such as price volatility, scalability issues, and environmental concerns related to the energy consumption required to operate the network.

Ultimately, Bitcoin has revolutionized the way we think about money and finance, paving the way for a new generation of cryptocurrencies and decentralized technologies.

Ethereum and Smart Contracts

Ethereum is an open-source public blockchain platform that was launched in 2015 by Vitalik Buterin, a Canadian developer. Ethereum is known as the second-largest cryptocurrency in terms of market capitalization after Bitcoin.

One of the main features that sets Ethereum apart from other cryptocurrencies is its support for «smart contracts.» Smart contracts are self-executing computer programs that automatically execute based on the terms and conditions defined in their code. They are designed to automate processes that are traditionally carried out manually, reducing costs and time.

Smart contracts are executed on the Ethereum blockchain, making them immutable, transparent, and resistant to censorship. This means that smart contracts can be used in a variety of fields, including finance, real estate, healthcare, energy, agriculture, and many more.

Ethereum is also known for being a more flexible platform than Bitcoin, as it supports various types of smart contracts and tokens. Ethereum has its own native currency called Ether (ETH), which is used to pay for transaction fees on the platform.

Ethereum smart contracts are written using a programming language called Solidity. Developers can use tools such as the Truffle development framework to facilitate the creation and deployment of smart contracts.

Ethereum smart contracts have also given rise to a growing ecosystem of decentralized projects and applications (dApps). These dApps are applications built on the Ethereum blockchain that utilize smart contracts to automate some of their functions.

Examples of dApps built on Ethereum include decentralized finance (DeFi) platforms like Uniswap, blockchain-based games like Axie Infinity, digital art auction platforms like OpenSea, and many more.

Altcoins: Diversity and Specificities

In the world of cryptocurrencies, altcoins refer to all cryptocurrencies other than Bitcoin. Since the creation of Bitcoin in 2009, thousands of altcoins have emerged, each with its own specificities and functionalities. The diversity of altcoins offers investors and users a multitude of options to engage in the world of cryptocurrencies.

Among the most well-known altcoins is Ethereum, created in 2015. Ethereum is an open-source platform that allows for the development of decentralized applications (dApps) and smart contracts, which are self-executing programs that automatically run when certain conditions are met. Ethereum is often considered the second most important cryptocurrency after Bitcoin in terms of market capitalization.

Another popular altcoin is Litecoin, created in 2011. Litecoin was designed to be a faster and lighter version of Bitcoin, with faster transaction confirmation times and a higher coin creation limit.

Ripple is another major altcoin that focuses on interbank transactions and cross-border fund transfers. The cryptocurrency was created to facilitate transactions between banks and other financial institutions, offering a fast and cost-effective alternative to traditional fund transfers.

There are also altcoins that are designed to be stable, meaning they are pegged to a fiat currency or an asset such as gold or oil. These altcoins are called stablecoins and are often used to protect investors from market volatility.

It is important to note that not all altcoins are created equal, and some may be riskier than others due to their lack of liquidity or low market capitalization. Therefore, it is essential for investors to conduct their own research and gather information about each altcoin before investing.

Stablecoins and CBDCs

Stablecoins and Central Bank Digital Currencies (CBDCs) are two types of cryptocurrencies that have gained popularity in recent years. Stablecoins are cryptocurrencies designed to maintain a stable value relative to another currency, such as the U.S. dollar. CBDCs are cryptocurrencies issued by central banks and intended to replace physical cash.

Stablecoins have become a popular alternative to volatile cryptocurrencies like Bitcoin. They are designed to be less volatile than other cryptocurrencies by maintaining a fixed parity with a fiat currency, such as the U.S. dollar. Stablecoins can be used for everyday transactions, investments, and international fund transfers.

Stablecoins are issued in various ways, but most of them utilize blockchain technology to store and manage transactions. Some stablecoins are backed by reserves of fiat currencies, meaning that each unit of the cryptocurrency is guaranteed by a unit of the corresponding fiat currency. Others use supply control mechanisms to maintain their parity, such as the burning or creation of additional tokens.

CBDCs, on the other hand, are cryptocurrencies issued by central banks to replace physical cash. CBDCs can be used for everyday transactions and value storage. CBDCs are designed to be faster, more efficient, and less costly than cash payments. Central banks can also use CBDCs to monitor and regulate economic activity.

CBDCs can be issued in various ways. Some central banks

have proposed issuing CBDCs fully backed by reserves of fiat currencies, while others have proposed CBDCs backed by assets. Some central banks have also proposed hybrid CBDCs that combine elements of both approaches.

Stablecoins and CBDCs have the potential to disrupt traditional financial systems. Stablecoins can provide an alternative to fiat currencies for international payments and everyday transactions. CBDCs can offer an alternative to physical cash, which can be costly and inefficient. However, their impact on traditional financial systems will depend on their adoption and regulation.

The Foundations of Cryptocurrencies

Wallets and Cryptographic Keys

Wallets, or «portefeuilles» in French, are computer applications that allow users to store, manage, and secure their cryptocurrencies. They come in different forms: software, hardware, or paper.

Software wallets are programs that can be installed on a computer, phone, or tablet. They are easy to use and allow users to manage their cryptocurrencies at any time. However, they are vulnerable to viruses and hacking attacks.

Hardware wallets are physical devices designed for managing cryptocurrencies. They come in the form of USB drives or small electronic devices. They are much more secure than software wallets because they allow users to store their private keys offline, away from hackers. However, they are more expensive than software wallets.

Paper wallets are printed sheets of paper that contain the private keys of cryptocurrencies. They are considered the most secure because they are disconnected from the internet and cannot be hacked. However, they are more difficult to use than software or hardware wallets.

Cryptographic keys are the codes that allow users to access the cryptocurrencies stored in a wallet. They consist of a public key and a private key. The public key is used to receive cryptocurrencies, while the private key is used to send them. It is therefore crucial to keep the private key safe, as it allows access to the funds stored in the wallet.

In summary, wallets and cryptographic keys are essential elements of cryptocurrency security and management. It is crucial to choose the right wallet based on one's needs and situation, and to keep the private keys safe to avoid the risk of hacking or theft.

Cryptography: Key Elements and Usage

Cryptography is one of the essential pillars of cryptocurrencies. Indeed, it is thanks to this discipline that transactions can be secured and users' privacy is preserved. Cryptography can be defined as the science of secret codes and secure communications. It has been used for millennia to protect sensitive information and state secrets. But how does cryptography work in the world of cryptocurrencies?

The key elements of cryptography in cryptocurrencies are public and private keys. Public keys are unique addresses that allow receiving payments, while private keys are passwords that allow signing transactions. Private keys are usually stored in secure electronic wallets, while public keys can be freely shared with other users.

Cryptography also allows verifying the integrity of transactions. Transactions are signed with private keys, ensuring that they have been made by the legitimate owner of the funds. Transactions are also encrypted using hash functions, ensuring that they cannot be modified once they have been sent.

Cryptography also ensures the confidentiality of transactions. Cryptocurrencies are often associated with privacy and anonymity, which means that users can make transactions without revealing their identity. To do this, transactions are typically mixed with other transactions to obscure their tracks.

It is important to understand that cryptography is not infallible and can be compromised if used improperly. For example, if private keys are lost or stolen, the funds associated with those keys can be lost forever. It is therefore essential to follow good security and storage practices to protect private keys.

Decentralized Networks and Resilience

Decentralized networks are a key characteristic of cryptocurrencies and blockchain technology. Unlike centralized systems, decentralized networks have no single point of control and are therefore less vulnerable to attacks and failures. Instead, transactions and operations are verified and validated by a large number of independent network nodes, ensuring greater transparency and security.

Resilience is also a key element of decentralized networks. In the event of a failure or attack, the network is capable of quickly and efficiently reorganizing itself thanks to its distributed structure. This resilience is strengthened by

the ability of network nodes to synchronize and cooperate
to maintain the security and validity of transactions.
Furthermore, the decentralized nature of networks allows
for greater user participation and autonomy in network
management.

However, despite these advantages, decentralized networks
can also present challenges. Their open and distributed
nature can lead to governance and coordination issues,
making it difficult to make important decisions or resolve
conflicts. Additionally, the number of network nodes can also
have an impact on network performance and scalability,
limiting its adoption on a large scale.

Despite these challenges, decentralized networks continue
to attract attention due to their transformative potential and
resilience in the face of external disruptions. By combining
the advantages of blockchain technology with a decentralized
structure, cryptocurrencies have the potential to create more
transparent, secure, and fair financial systems.

Monetary Issuance and Inflation Control

Cryptocurrencies are often presented as an alternative to
traditional currencies. One of the most significant differences
between these two types of currencies is their method of
monetary issuance and inflation control.

In traditional currencies, central banks have the power
to create and circulate money based on the state of the
economy. This is often done through monetary policies aimed

at stimulating economic activity or curbing inflation.

In cryptocurrencies, on the other hand, the issuance of new units of currency is typically programmed and predictable. This method is called «mining» in the case of Bitcoin, and it involves solving complex mathematical problems to validate transactions and add new blocks to the blockchain. In reward for this work, miners receive new units of currency.

This method of creating money may seem strange to people accustomed to traditional currencies. However, it has several advantages. First, it makes monetary issuance predictable and transparent, which can help maintain users' confidence in the currency. Additionally, it prevents central banks or governments from creating money at will, which can lead to currency devaluation and inflation.

However, the mining method is not without flaws. First, it is very energy-intensive and can have a significant environmental impact. Additionally, it can lead to a concentration of currency production in the hands of a few powerful miners. This can make the cryptocurrency less decentralized and more vulnerable to malicious attacks.

Finally, it is worth noting that cryptocurrencies are not immune to inflation. Although monetary issuance is predictable, the value of the currency can fluctuate based on demand and supply in the markets. Additionally, the creation of new cryptocurrencies can dilute the value of those already in circulation.

Transactions and Fees

One of the key advantages of cryptocurrencies is the speed and ease with which transactions can be conducted. Transactions are made by sending units of the cryptocurrency from the sender to the recipient, via the blockchain. Transactions are verified by miners, who are rewarded with new units of the cryptocurrency for their work.

However, transactions are not free. Each transaction must pay fees to cover the cost of verification and inclusion on the blockchain. Fees are determined by the size of the transaction in bytes and are paid using the cryptocurrency of the transaction itself. Generally, the larger the transaction size, the higher the fees.

The cost of transaction fees is often very low compared to the traditional transaction fees associated with banks and other financial institutions. However, it is important to note that transaction fees can vary significantly depending on the cryptocurrency used, the size of the transaction, and current demand for transactions.

Transaction fees can also be influenced by the monetary policy of the cryptocurrency in question. For example, Bitcoin has a limited number of available blocks for transactions, which means that fees can increase when demand for transactions rises.

It is important to note that transaction fees are not the only cost associated with cryptocurrencies. Users must also consider the costs associated with owning and managing a cryptocurrency wallet, as well as the costs of converting to fiat currency if necessary.

Addresses and Electronic Wallets

Addresses and electronic wallets are essential elements of the cryptocurrency ecosystem. Addresses are alphanumeric strings used to identify the origin and destination of transactions on the blockchain. Electronic wallets are software programs that allow users to store, send, and receive cryptocurrencies.

There are several types of addresses and electronic wallets, each with its advantages and disadvantages. Addresses can be Bitcoin, Ethereum, or other cryptocurrency addresses and can be generated online or offline. Electronic wallets can be hardware wallets or software wallets, with significant differences in terms of security and ease of use.

Software wallets can be divided into two categories: online wallets (hot wallets) and offline wallets (cold wallets). Online wallets are electronic wallets accessible from a web browser or mobile application, while offline wallets are physical devices not connected to the internet.

Hardware wallets are considered the most secure because they store private keys offline and provide additional security against viruses and hacking attacks. Popular hardware wallets include Ledger, Trezor, and KeepKey. Popular software wallets include Exodus, MyEtherWallet, and Coinbase.

It is important to note that electronic wallets do not store cryptocurrencies themselves, but only the private keys needed to access funds on the blockchain. Therefore, the security of these keys is crucial to the security of the funds. It is recommended to store private keys offline, in a safe place protected by strong passwords.

The underlying technology: blockchain

Blockchain: definition, functioning, and applications

Blockchain is a key concept in the world of cryptocurrencies and decentralized technology. It can be defined as a decentralized and secure digital ledger, where transactions are recorded and verified by a network of participants rather than a central authority. This allows for transparency and immutability of data, which are essential characteristics for many applications.

The functioning of blockchain can be compared to a public register, where each transaction is recorded in a block. Each block is then added to a chain of blocks in a chronological and secure manner using cryptography. To add a new block to the chain, a network of participants must solve a complex mathematical problem, known as the «consensus mechanism».

Blockchain can be used in many fields, including decentralized finance (DeFi), supply chain management, intellectual property, smart contracts, and much more. Transactions can be conducted faster, cheaper, and more securely than traditional methods.

For example, in the field of DeFi, users can exchange cryptocurrencies, lend and borrow, while maintaining full control over their assets. Blockchain-based smart contracts also allow for the establishment of autonomous and programmable agreements between parties.

It is important to note that blockchain is not a perfect solution and it also presents challenges. For example, scalability is a major issue as the number of transactions that can be processed per second is limited. Additionally, security must be constantly improved to prevent hacking and fraud.

The structure of blockchains: chains, trees, and graphs

The structure of blockchains is a key concept in understanding the underlying technology of cryptocurrencies. Blockchains are digital transaction registers, stored in real-time on decentralized networks of nodes (computers) that verify and validate transactions. The security and integrity of data in blockchains are guaranteed through the use of cryptography and consensus mechanisms.

There are several types of blockchain structures, including chains, trees, and graphs. Chain blockchains are the simplest and most common form of blockchain. Transactions are recorded in blocks that are then added to a linear chain of blocks. Each new block is linked to the previous one, hence the term blockchain.

Tree blockchains are similar to chain blockchains but with branches. Transactions are recorded in blocks that are then linked to other blocks to form branches of the blockchain.

Tree blockchains are often used to solve scalability issues as they allow for processing more transactions in parallel.

Graph blockchains are the most complex as they allow for transactions between multiple blocks. Transactions are recorded in blocks that can be linked to other blocks to form a network of interconnected blocks. Graph blockchains are often used for DeFi applications that require complex smart contracts.

Different blockchain architectures

Blockchain is the underlying technology for all cryptocurrencies, and it is designed to be decentralized, transparent, and secure. However, there are different blockchain architectures, each with its own advantages and disadvantages.

Public blockchains are the most well-known, as they are used for most cryptocurrencies such as Bitcoin and Ethereum. In a public blockchain, all transactions are public and verifiable by everyone, making the system transparent and resistant to fraud. Miners are responsible for verifying and approving transactions, and they are rewarded for their work through the creation of new units of cryptocurrencies.

Private blockchains, on the other hand, are reserved for a specific group of users and are not accessible to the general public. They are often used for industrial and financial applications that require a high level of security and privacy.

Hybrid blockchains combine the characteristics of public and private blockchains, allowing some users to participate in the transaction validation process while keeping certain information confidential.

Consortium blockchains are private blockchains controlled by a group of selected participants, such as banks or companies, who work together to validate transactions and ensure the security of the system.

Lastly, interoperable blockchains are blockchains that can communicate with each other, allowing users to transfer assets between different blockchains without intermediaries.

Each of these blockchain architectures has its advantages and disadvantages. Public blockchains offer transparency and maximum security, but they can be very slow and consume a lot of energy. Private and hybrid blockchains, on the other hand, offer greater privacy and control, but they may be less secure and less resistant to fraud.

Ultimately, the choice of blockchain architecture will depend on the specific needs of each project or application. It is important to understand the advantages and disadvantages of each blockchain architecture in order to choose the best one for your project.

Public, private, hybrid, and consortium blockchains

Blockchains are distributed ledgers that allow for recording and securing transactions without relying on a central authority. These blockchains can be public, private, hybrid, or consortium.

Public blockchains, such as Bitcoin, are accessible to everyone and transparent. They operate with decentralized consensus protocols such as Proof of Work or Proof of Stake. Transactions are validated by miners who are rewarded in cryptocurrencies for their work.

Private blockchains are used by organizations or businesses for internal transactions. They are controlled by a central authority that can decide who can access and participate in them. Private blockchains are faster and more efficient than public blockchains, but they are less transparent and less decentralized.

Hybrid blockchains combine elements of public and private blockchains. They allow for some transparency while ensuring a certain level of confidentiality. Hybrid blockchains are used in cases where transparency is needed for some parties, but privacy is important for others.

Consortium blockchains are private blockchains used by a group of participants who have a common interest. Consortium blockchains are often used in sectors such as finance, logistics, and health, where multiple actors need to work together to perform transactions.

Interoperable blockchains and multi-chain systems

Blockchain technology has revolutionized the finance world by offering a decentralized alternative to traditional financial systems. However, blockchains have often operated in isolation without interacting with each other. This has led to market fragmentation and difficulty for users to exchange digital assets between different blockchains. Interoperable blockchains have been created to address this issue.

An interoperable blockchain is a blockchain capable of communicating with other blockchains, regardless of their architecture. Interoperable blockchains allow users to transfer assets from one blockchain to another without relying on centralized exchanges and without incurring high fees. Interoperable blockchains also enable the development of inter-chain decentralized applications, where data can be shared among multiple blockchains, offering more advanced functionalities than decentralized applications on a single blockchain.

There are several solutions for interoperable blockchains, including Cosmos, Polkadot, ICON, Aion, Wanchain, and Ark. These solutions are based on standardized communication protocols, such as Interledger, that allow blockchains to communicate with each other. Interoperable solutions can be implemented at multiple levels, including protocol level, application level, and service level.

Multi-chain systems are another solution to enable interoperability between blockchains. Multi-chain systems are networks of interconnected blockchains that can work together seamlessly. Multi-chain systems allow users to transfer assets from one blockchain to another without relying on centralized exchanges and without incurring high fees.

Examples of multi-chain systems include Polkadot and Cosmos. Polkadot uses a relay chain architecture to connect multiple blockchains together and enable communication between them. Cosmos, on the other hand, uses a hub and zone architecture to facilitate communication between different blockchains.

Use cases and application domains

There are numerous use cases and application domains for cryptocurrencies, and they continue to expand. Although their adoption is still relatively limited in some sectors, cryptocurrencies are changing the way we perceive financial transactions and the exchange of goods and services.

The most obvious application domain is payments, where cryptocurrencies offer a digital alternative to traditional payment methods such as credit cards and bank transfers. Cryptocurrencies enable near-instant, low-cost, and secure transactions worldwide. For example, platforms like BitPay allow businesses to accept payments in Bitcoin, Ethereum, Bitcoin Cash, and many other cryptocurrencies.

Cryptocurrencies have also found use cases in the logistics and supply chain sector, where transparency and traceability are essential. Blockchain technology allows for the complete tracking of transaction and movement history of goods, from production to delivery, including warehousing and distribution. For example, Blockshipping is developing a blockchain-based container tracking platform.

Another booming application domain is decentralized finance (DeFi), which aims to create an open and accessible financial system without intermediaries or central institutions. DeFi protocols allow users to lend, borrow, trade, and stake cryptocurrencies without relying on banks or brokers. Popular DeFi platforms include Uniswap, Aave, Compound, and MakerDAO.

Cryptocurrencies have also been adopted in the art and culture sector, particularly with the emergence of non-fungible tokens (NFTs). NFTs are unique tokens created on the blockchain that represent digital ownership of assets such as artworks, videos, and games. NFTs offer content creators a new way to monetize their work, and buyers a way to own unique and authenticated digital assets. Popular NFT platforms include OpenSea, SuperRare, and Nifty Gateway.

Finally, cryptocurrencies have found use cases in developing countries where access to traditional financial services is often limited. Cryptocurrencies allow millions of people to benefit from basic banking services such as payments, money transfers, and savings. For example, the mobile payment platform BitPesa enables users to perform Bitcoin transactions in Kenya, Tanzania, and Uganda.

Consensus Mechanisms and Security

Consensus: Proof of Work, Proof of Stake, and Alternatives

Cryptocurrencies are based on decentralized networks that operate through consensus mechanisms. These mechanisms validate transactions on the network and ensure the integrity of the blockchain.

Proof of Work (PoW) is the consensus mechanism used by the first cryptocurrency, Bitcoin. Miners solve complex mathematical problems to validate transactions and add blocks to the blockchain. However, this process is energy-intensive, as it requires powerful computers to solve the mathematical problems. Additionally, Proof of Work makes the network more vulnerable to 51% attacks.

Proof of Stake (PoS) is an alternative to Proof of Work that reduces energy consumption. In this mechanism, validators are chosen based on the amount of cryptocurrency they hold and stake as collateral. Validators are then rewarded for validating transactions on the network. Proof of Stake also reduces the risk of 51% attacks.

There are also other consensus mechanisms, such as Proof of Authority (PoA) and Proof of Space-Time (PoST).

The choice of consensus mechanism depends on the

objectives and characteristics of each cryptocurrency. Proof of Work is generally used for cryptocurrencies that prioritize security and decentralization, while Proof of Stake is used for cryptocurrencies aiming to reduce energy consumption and accelerate transactions.

The Challenges of Decentralization and Trust

Decentralization and trust are at the core of cryptocurrencies. Cryptocurrencies are digital currencies regulated by decentralized networks rather than central financial institutions like banks. Decentralized networks are created by a set of nodes that work together to maintain transaction validity using blockchain technology.

One of the main advantages of decentralization is increased security. Data stored on a decentralized network is harder to hack or manipulate, as the data is duplicated and stored on multiple different nodes. Therefore, even if one node is compromised, the other nodes in the network can continue to function normally.

Furthermore, decentralization allows for greater transparency, as all transactions are recorded on a public ledger called the blockchain. This means that all transactions are verifiable and traceable, making it more difficult to falsify or manipulate data. Users can trust the system because they know that all transactions are recorded transparently and immutably.

However, decentralization can also pose challenges in terms of governance and regulation. Since there is no central authority to regulate the network, it is important to find ways to make collective decisions. Decentralized governance, based on consensus protocols such as Proof of Work or Proof of Stake, can help address these challenges.

Trust is also a key element of decentralization. Cryptocurrencies are often seen as a way to bypass traditional financial institutions and give individuals greater control over their money. However, for this to be possible, users must trust the system. They must be convinced that their money is secure and that they can access their funds at any time.

Security is therefore an essential aspect of trust. Users need to know that their funds are secure and that they can access their wallets at all times. Cryptocurrency wallets provide a high level of security by using cryptographic keys to secure funds. However, this also means that users are responsible for the security of their own funds, which can be a challenge for those unfamiliar with technology.

Finally, trust in cryptocurrencies also depends on their adoption by businesses and consumers. The more companies that accept cryptocurrency payments, the easier it will be for users to purchase goods and services with their funds. Governments and financial institutions can also play a key role in building trust by providing a stable regulatory framework and encouraging technology adoption.

Consensus Protocols: Proof of Work, Proof of Stake, etc.

Consensus protocols are algorithms that allow participants in the network to reach consensus on the state of the system and valid transactions. The consensus protocol is a key element of blockchain technology, as it ensures the security and reliability of the network.

The most well-known consensus protocol is Proof of Work (PoW), used by Bitcoin and many other cryptocurrencies. PoW relies on miners solving complex mathematical problems and is rewarded with new tokens. This process requires high energy consumption, as miners need to perform intensive calculations to solve the equations.

Another consensus protocol is Proof of Stake (PoS), used by cryptocurrencies like Cardano and Ethereum. Unlike PoW, PoS does not require intensive calculations, but relies on staking a certain amount of tokens. Validators of the network are selected based on the amount of tokens they have staked, giving participants an incentive to maintain the integrity of the network.

Other emerging consensus protocols include Delegated Proof of Stake (DPoS), Proof of Authority (PoA), and Proof of Elapsed Time (PoET). Each of these protocols has its advantages and disadvantages in terms of security, scalability, and energy efficiency.

In general, consensus protocols are designed to address the challenges of coordination and trust in a decentralized system. Consensus protocols enable participants to reach agreement on the state of the system without relying on a central entity. However, each protocol has its own challenges and trade-offs, and developers must take these factors into account when designing cryptocurrency networks.

Consensus Mechanisms and Their Pros and Cons

Consensus mechanisms are at the heart of cryptocurrencies and are essential to ensuring their security and operation. These mechanisms validate transactions on the blockchain and ensure the consistency and integrity of the network.

There are different consensus mechanisms, each with its own pros and cons. The first consensus mechanism used is Proof of Work (PoW), which is used by Bitcoin. PoW involves solving complex mathematical calculations to validate transactions and create new blocks. Miners who solve these calculations are rewarded with new cryptocurrency units.

The main advantage of PoW is its security, as it is very difficult for an attacker to alter existing blocks without being detected. However, PoW is also energy-intensive because the calculations require significant computational power, which can make the transaction validation process slow and costly.

Another consensus mechanism is Proof of Stake (PoS), used by cryptocurrencies such as Cardano and Ethereum. In PoS, validators (or «stakers») must prove their commitment to the blockchain by locking a certain amount of tokens. Validators are selected based on the number of tokens they have locked and are rewarded with transaction fees.

The main advantage of PoS is its reduced energy consumption compared to PoW, as there are no complex mathematical calculations to solve. However, some critics argue that PoS favors large token holders, which can lead to centralization of the network.

There are also other consensus mechanisms such as Proof of Capacity (PoC), Proof of Work and Service (PoWS), and Proof of Participation (PoP), but they are less commonly used.

Challenges and Solutions in Security

Security is one of the major challenges in the world of cryptocurrencies, as the decentralized nature of blockchains makes them potentially vulnerable to various malicious attacks. Cryptocurrency holders must therefore be particularly vigilant about the security of their digital assets.

One of the most common risks is wallet hacking, where an attacker seeks to gain access to the private keys of a wallet to seize the funds. Users must take security measures to protect their private keys, such as using hardware wallets or enabling two-factor authentication.

Another threat is the possibility of a 51% attack, where a group of attackers can take control of more than half of a blockchain's computational power, allowing them to manipulate transactions and falsify the blockchain. Proof of

Work and Proof of Stake consensus protocols are designed to prevent this type of attack, but it is important to monitor the distribution of computational power on a given blockchain to detect any anomalies.

Exchange hacks, where trading platforms are compromised, can also result in loss of funds. Users must choose reputable and reliable exchange platforms and ensure that their funds are securely stored.

It is also important to note that cryptocurrency security is closely related to general computer security. Users must take security measures such as using strong passwords and up-to-date antivirus software to protect against cyberattacks.

There are also solutions to strengthen the security of cryptocurrencies. For example, blockchains can be designed to incorporate privacy and data protection features to protect users against surveillance and data theft attacks.

Alternative consensus protocols, such as Proof of Authority and Proof of Reputation, are also being developed to enhance security and prevent attacks.

Lastly, the adoption of regulations and security standards for the cryptocurrency industry can help protect users from risks and build trust in cryptocurrencies.

Overall, security is a major challenge for cryptocurrencies, but there are measures that users can take to protect themselves and solutions being developed to enhance the security of the entire industry. It is important to take appropriate security measures to safeguard digital assets and stay informed about security developments in the world of cryptocurrencies.

Protocols and Exchange Platforms

Decentralized Exchange Protocols

Decentralized exchange protocols represent a major innovation in the world of cryptocurrencies. They allow users to trade crypto assets directly with each other, without relying on a centralized exchange platform.

Unlike centralized exchange platforms, decentralized exchange protocols are built on blockchain technology and are completely transparent and public. Users can securely exchange crypto assets without having to trust a third party. Additionally, they are not restricted by geographic or currency limitations imposed by centralized exchange platforms.

Decentralized exchange protocols also provide better protection against the risks of hacking and fund theft, as funds are stored directly in the user's wallet and not on a centralized server. Furthermore, transaction fees are often lower on decentralized exchange protocols compared to centralized exchange platforms.

There are several popular decentralized exchange protocols, such as Uniswap, SushiSwap, and PancakeSwap. These protocols are built on public blockchains like Ethereum and Binance Smart Chain, and allow users to easily trade crypto assets.

However, decentralized exchange protocols also have some drawbacks. For example, liquidity on these protocols can be limited, which can result in significant price differences compared to centralized exchange platforms. Additionally, the complexity of using decentralized exchange protocols can discourage beginners or less tech-savvy users.

Despite these limitations, decentralized exchange protocols represent an important innovation in the world of cryptocurrencies. They offer users a safer, more transparent, and more accessible way to trade crypto assets, and are an example of the power of blockchain technology in reshaping the rules of the game in the financial world.

Centralized Exchange Platforms

Centralized exchange platforms are websites where users can exchange cryptocurrencies for other assets or currencies, and where the exchanges are facilitated by a trusted third party, typically the exchange platform operator. These platforms were the first major players in the cryptocurrency ecosystem and continue to play an important role for users looking to invest or trade cryptocurrencies.

Centralized exchange platforms generally offer simple and user-friendly interfaces, allowing users to buy or sell cryptocurrencies with fiat currencies or other cryptocurrencies. Users can place buy or sell orders at specific prices, and exchanges are executed as soon as offers and demands meet. Centralized exchange platforms also provide advanced trading tools for more experienced users, such as price charts, technical indicators, and fundamental analysis tools.

However, centralized exchange platforms also face major challenges in terms of security and reliability. Exchange platforms have been targeted in several hacking attacks over the years, resulting in the loss of millions of dollars of customer funds. Additionally, some exchange platforms have been accused of manipulating prices and engaging in deceptive trading practices.

These risks have led many users to turn to decentralized exchange platforms, which operate without a trusted intermediary and offer a higher level of security due to their distributed architecture. However, centralized exchange platforms remain a popular option for many users, due to their user-friendliness and high liquidity.

It is important to note that users should always exercise caution when using centralized exchange platforms and take appropriate security measures to protect their funds. This may include using two-factor authentication, storing funds in offline cold wallets, and verifying the reputation and track record of the exchange platform before trusting it with funds.

Market Liquidity and Transparency

Market liquidity and transparency are key elements in the functioning of cryptocurrencies. Liquidity refers to the ease with which a cryptocurrency can be bought or sold on a market. Good liquidity allows investors to buy or sell cryptocurrencies without having to wait long to find a buyer or seller. Transparency, on the other hand, refers to the visibility of transactions and fund movements on a market. It allows investors to track price movements and assess the risk associated with an investment.

Market liquidity and transparency largely depend on the market size and number of participants. Popular cryptocurrencies like Bitcoin and Ethereum generally have better liquidity than lesser-known cryptocurrencies. Centralized exchange platforms like Binance, Coinbase, and Kraken are the largest marketplaces for cryptocurrencies, offering high liquidity and high transparency due to the visibility of their order books.

However, transparency can be compromised if malicious actors seek to manipulate the market. This can happen if a large investor buys or sells a large amount of cryptocurrencies at once, which can cause price fluctuations and deceive investors. Decentralized exchanges are often considered more transparent as they operate without intermediaries, but their liquidity is often lower than that of centralized exchanges.

Market liquidity and transparency can also be affected by government regulations. If a country bans the use or trading of cryptocurrencies, it can reduce liquidity and transparency of that cryptocurrency in that country. Regulatory restrictions can also make it difficult for investors to find reliable exchanges to buy or sell cryptocurrencies.

Key Players in the Cryptocurrency Market

Miners and Network Nodes

Cryptocurrencies are decentralized digital currencies that are created, stored, and transferred through a network of participants known as the blockchain. This network is managed by miners and nodes who work together to ensure the security and validity of transactions.

Miners are network participants who use their computational power to verify transactions and create new blocks of transactions. Each block contains recent transactions that have been verified by miners and added to the blockchain. As a reward for their work, miners receive a small amount of the currently being created cryptocurrency.

Nodes are network participants who store a copy of the blockchain and verify the transactions added to it. Nodes are essential for network security as they verify the validity of transactions before they are added to the blockchain. In case of doubt, nodes can reject a suspicious transaction and prevent fraud.

It is important to note that not all miners are nodes, and not all nodes are miners. Miners are responsible for creating new blocks of transactions and validating the transactions added to them, while nodes are responsible for storing and verifying the transactions that have been added to the blockchain.

Creating new blocks of transactions is a process that requires a significant amount of computational power. This means that miners must invest in expensive computer hardware to participate in the creation of new blocks. This can make the mining process highly competitive, as miners with the most powerful resources are often more likely to create new blocks and receive a reward.

Trading Platforms and Brokerage Services

Trading platforms and brokerage services are key elements of the cryptocurrency ecosystem. These platforms allow users to buy, sell, and trade cryptocurrencies for traditional currencies such as the euro or the dollar. Brokerage services, on the other hand, offer similar services but are often associated with advisory and portfolio management offerings.

Exchange platforms can be centralized or decentralized. Centralized exchange platforms are often more user-friendly and offer advanced features such as the use of financial leverage for investment. However, they also present risks such as data or fund hacks. Decentralized exchange platforms are safer as they are based on blockchain technologies but may be more challenging for beginners to use.

Brokerage services are an interesting option for those looking to invest in cryptocurrencies but lack technical knowledge or need assistance in managing their portfolio. These services offer analysis tools and personalized advice to help investors make informed decisions based on their investment goals.

It is important to choose the right exchange platform or brokerage service by taking into account various criteria such as transaction fees, security, liquidity, product range, and offered services. It is also important to verify the reputation and track record of the platform or brokerage service from reliable sources.

Finally, it is important to emphasize that the use of exchange platforms or brokerage services does not guarantee profitability in cryptocurrency investments. Investors should always exercise caution and due diligence in their investment decisions and never invest more than they can afford to lose.

Storage and Wallet Management Service Providers

Storage and wallet management service providers are key players in the cryptocurrency ecosystem. They offer solutions for securely storing and managing digital assets.

There are two types of storage: hot storage and cold storage. Hot storage involves storing cryptocurrencies on web-connected electronic wallets, making them more vulnerable to hacks. Cold storage, on the other hand, involves storing digital assets offline on physical media such as encrypted USB drives or external hard drives. This storage method is considered the most secure.

Cryptocurrency storage service providers offer a range of hot and cold storage solutions to meet their clients' needs. They also provide electronic wallet management solutions, which allow users to track the movement of their digital assets and easily manage them.

Storage and wallet management service providers are regulated and must comply with current security standards to ensure the safety of their clients' digital assets. Some market players, such as banks, are also entering the provision of cryptocurrency storage and wallet management services.

Cryptocurrency Platforms and Services

Exchanges: Centralized and Decentralized

One key aspect of the cryptocurrency world is the ability for users to exchange digital currencies. Exchanges are online platforms that allow users to buy, sell, and trade cryptocurrencies in real time. There are two types of cryptocurrency exchanges: centralized and decentralized.

Centralized exchanges are platforms that function like traditional stock exchanges, with a company at the helm managing operations and ensuring fund security. Users can deposit funds into the exchange, which are then used to buy cryptocurrencies on the platform. Centralized exchanges are often more user-friendly for beginners, as they offer comprehensive customer service and technical support. Centralized exchanges are also more liquid, meaning there are more buyers and sellers, facilitating the trading of digital currencies.

However, centralized exchanges are also more vulnerable to hacking attacks, as all funds are stored in a single centralized entity. There have been several instances in the past of centralized exchanges being hacked, resulting in the loss of millions of dollars of user funds. Centralized exchanges are also subject to stricter government regulation, as they are considered traditional financial entities.

Decentralized exchanges, on the other hand, are platforms that operate without a central authority or company at the helm. Users can directly trade cryptocurrencies with each other, using a blockchain to record transactions. Decentralized exchanges are more secure, as user funds are stored in their own wallets rather than on a centralized platform. Decentralized exchanges are also more transparent, as all transactions are recorded on a public blockchain.

However, decentralized exchanges are often less user-friendly for beginners, as they require some technical knowledge of blockchain and cryptocurrency wallets. Decentralized exchanges can also be less liquid, making the trading of cryptocurrencies more challenging.

Ultimately, the choice between a centralized or decentralized exchange will depend on the preferences and priorities of each user. Centralized exchanges offer greater ease of use and liquidity, but are more vulnerable to hacking attacks. Decentralized exchanges are safer and more transparent, but can be more complex to use and less liquid. Both types of exchanges have advantages and disadvantages, and users must conduct their own research to decide which type of exchange best suits their needs and goals.

Lending and Staking Platforms

Lending and staking platforms are key elements of the cryptocurrency ecosystem. They allow cryptocurrency holders to earn interest on their holdings while providing a source of funding for borrowers. These platforms are often used in the context of decentralized finance (DeFi), which aims to offer more accessible and equitable financial services to all.

Lending platforms function by connecting borrowers and lenders in a decentralized manner. Borrowers provide cryptocurrency collateral to obtain loans, while lenders provide cryptocurrency liquidity to generate interest on their investment. The interest rates offered by these platforms vary depending on supply and demand, as well as the level of risk associated with each borrower.

Staking platforms, on the other hand, allow cryptocurrency holders to participate in transaction validation on a blockchain network. By staking their tokens, they contribute to the security and resilience of the network and receive rewards in the form of new units of cryptocurrency. Staking is also a form of participation in network governance, as token holders often have the right to vote on important decisions.

These platforms can be used by cryptocurrency holders of all types, whether individuals or institutions. They also offer flexibility in terms of investment duration, interest rates, and risk level. Lending and staking platforms have become very popular in recent years, thanks to the growth of DeFi and the increase in the number of cryptocurrency investors.

However, it is important to note that these platforms also present risks. Fluctuations in cryptocurrency prices can affect the value of collateral provided by borrowers, and interest rates offered by platforms can vary significantly depending on supply and demand. Investors must therefore be aware of these risks and exercise diligence when using these platforms.

Decentralized Applications (dApps)

Decentralized applications (dApps) are computer programs designed to run on blockchain technology, which forms the basis of cryptocurrencies. Unlike traditional applications that are controlled by a central authority, dApps are decentralized, meaning they are executed on a network of nodes that are independent of each other.

dApps can take many forms, ranging from games to financial applications, social networks, and file-sharing platforms. What sets them apart from traditional applications is that they are built on decentralized and autonomous protocols, allowing them to offer unique advantages such as transparency, security, and resilience.

dApps are often associated with DeFi protocols, as they offer financial solutions without the need for intermediation from traditional financial institutions. For example, dApps such as Uniswap allow users to directly exchange cryptocurrencies without relying on a centralized exchange platform. Similarly, decentralized lending protocols such as Aave enable users to lend and borrow cryptocurrencies without relying on a traditional bank.

dApps can also offer advantages for content creators by allowing the creation and distribution of decentralized content without relying on centralized platforms like YouTube or Vimeo. For example, dApps like BitTube offer decentralized video-sharing platforms that allow users to earn cryptocurrency rewards for content creation.

Oracles and Data Aggregation Services

Oracles and data aggregation services are key elements of the cryptocurrency ecosystem. Oracles are interfaces that connect real-world data with smart contracts executed on the blockchain. They are essential for dApps to interact with real-time information such as asset prices, weather data, or news events.

Data aggregation services, on the other hand, are platforms that gather and provide high-quality data from different sources, allowing users to make informed investment decisions. These services are often used by traders to obtain information on trading volumes, prices, market trends, and trading signals.

Oracles and data aggregation services are crucial for the cryptocurrency ecosystem, as they enable dApps to function properly and provide users with valuable information for their investment decisions.

However, oracles and data aggregation services are also subject to risks such as data errors, data manipulation, and malicious attacks. To address these issues, security solutions such as cryptography, consensus mechanisms, and security audits are used to ensure the integrity and confidentiality of data.

Ultimately, oracles and data aggregation services are indispensable tools for dApps and investors in the cryptocurrency world. They bridge the gap between the real world and the blockchain, providing quality information for informed decision-making. However, it is important to use them with caution and consider the potential risks associated with these services.

Cryptocurrencies and Technical Challenges

Scalability and Solutions for Improving Network Performance

Scalability is one of the major challenges faced by cryptocurrencies. As the popularity of cryptocurrencies increases, the number of transactions processed on blockchain networks also increases, which can lead to bottlenecks and longer processing times.

Fortunately, several solutions have been proposed to improve the scalability of cryptocurrencies. One of the most common solutions is optimizing consensus protocols, such as proof of work and proof of stake. These protocols are essential for validating transactions on the network and need to be efficient to avoid prolonged processing times.

Another popular solution for improving scalability is the use of off-chain scaling technology, such as the Lightning Network for Bitcoin. This technology allows for off-chain transactions, reducing the number of transactions processed on the main chain and improving processing times.

Sharding networks are also a promising solution for improving the scalability of cryptocurrencies. This technology involves splitting the database into multiple fragments, called shards, that can be processed in parallel. This allows for faster processing of a greater number of transactions without sacrificing network security.

Lastly, the adoption of alternative consensus protocols, such as Delegated Proof of Stake (DPoS), can also contribute to improving the scalability of cryptocurrencies. DPoS protocols allow token holders to vote for the nodes that will validate transactions on the network, reducing the number of nodes required for validation.

Privacy and Anonymity Challenges

Privacy and anonymity are key issues in the world of cryptocurrencies. Unlike traditional financial transactions, cryptocurrency transactions are often anonymous and do not require the identification of parties involved. This characteristic can be both a strength and a weakness of cryptocurrencies.

On one hand, transaction anonymity can be seen as a major advancement for user privacy. Cryptocurrency transactions can be conducted without disclosing personal information, which is particularly important for individuals seeking to protect their privacy. Additionally, this can also make transactions more secure, as personal information is not exposed to hacking risks.

However, transaction anonymity can also be exploited for illegal purposes, such as money laundering and financing terrorism. Regulators and authorities tend to view this anonymity as a weakness of cryptocurrencies, as it can facilitate criminal activities.

To address these challenges, many cryptocurrencies now incorporate enhanced privacy features. For example, some cryptocurrencies use advanced encryption techniques to protect personal data, while others implement mixing techniques to make transactions more difficult to trace. Furthermore, regulators are starting to take measures to limit transaction anonymity in cryptocurrencies, which can help prevent illegal activities.

Interoperability Issues and Communication Protocols

Interoperability is a major challenge for cryptocurrencies. The lack of standardization in communication protocols between different cryptocurrency networks can make interaction and value exchange between them difficult.

To solve this problem, several projects have been developed to enable efficient interoperability. One of the most well-known is the Cosmos project, which aims to create an ecosystem of interoperable blockchains. Cosmos relies on the creation of a protocol called Tendermint, which allows for the creation of blockchains compatible with the Cosmos network. These blockchains can then communicate with each other through a communication protocol called Inter-Blockchain Communication (IBC).

Another important project in this field is Polkadot, which is based on a umbrella-shaped network architecture, with a central blockchain (Polkadot) and several satellite blockchains (parachains). These parachains can specialize in specific application domains (e.g., gaming) and can communicate with each other through a protocol called Cross-Chain Message Passing (XCMP).

It is also worth mentioning the Chainlink project, which aims to connect blockchains to real-world data (e.g., weather data or exchange rates). Chainlink uses «oracles», agents that retrieve real-world data and transmit it to smart contracts on blockchains.

Lastly, it is important to note that research on interoperability is still ongoing, and many emerging projects are attempting to tackle this challenge. For example, the RenVM project aims to create an interoperability solution for privacy coins (such as Bitcoin or Zcash), while the Wanchain project aims to create an interoperability solution for Ethereum-based blockchains.

Decentralized Finance (DeFi)

Principles and Benefits of DeFi

Decentralized Finance (DeFi) is an emerging category of blockchain technology that offers alternative and decentralized financial solutions. It utilizes blockchain to create a financial ecosystem that does not rely on traditional intermediaries such as banks, brokers, and insurance companies. The fundamental principles of DeFi are transparency, security, accessibility, and openness.

One of the main advantages of DeFi is that it allows users to bypass traditional financial services by offering low-cost and accessible alternatives. Users can participate in DeFi as lenders, borrowers, or liquidity providers. DeFi can also provide financial services to people who do not have access to traditional banking services or have difficulty obtaining loans from traditional financial institutions.

Another advantage of DeFi is that it enables total transparency of transactions. All transactions are recorded on the blockchain and are accessible to all users. This provides better security, as all transactions are verified and validated by network users, reducing the risks of fraud and corruption.

DeFi also offers more efficient and faster lending solutions than traditional loans by eliminating intermediaries and enabling peer-to-peer lending. The interest rates offered by DeFi protocols are often lower than those of traditional financial institutions, allowing users to achieve significant savings.

Lastly, DeFi also allows for great flexibility in asset utilization. Users can use a wide variety of cryptocurrencies as collateral for loans, and can also use traditional assets such as fiat currencies. This offers a diverse range of investment options for users.

Exchange and Liquidity Protocols

Exchange and liquidity protocols are key components of the cryptocurrency market. They enable investors to buy, sell, and trade digital assets quickly and efficiently, which is essential for market growth and stability. In this section, we will explore the different exchange and liquidity protocols that exist, as well as centralized and decentralized exchange platforms.

Decentralized exchange protocols (DEXs) have gained popularity in recent years as they offer investors a safer and more transparent way to trade digital assets. Unlike centralized exchanges, DEXs do not rely on a single entity for storing and processing transactions, reducing the risk of hacking and theft. DEXs use smart contracts to automate transactions between buyers and sellers, without the need for a centralized intermediary. This reduces transaction fees and ensures greater transparency in transactions.

Centralized exchange platforms, on the other hand, are still very popular among investors. They offer higher liquidity than DEXs, allowing traders to buy and sell digital assets quickly and easily. However, centralized exchanges are more exposed to risks of hacking and theft, as they rely on a single access point for storing and processing transactions.

Centralized exchange platforms also offer additional features, such as the ability to purchase digital assets with fiat currencies (such as the US dollar or the euro), as well as the ability to use market analysis tools and portfolio tracking.

Both types of exchange platforms have advantages and disadvantages. DEXs are safer and more transparent, but have lower liquidity. Centralized exchanges offer higher liquidity but are more exposed to risks of hacking and theft. Investors must therefore consider these factors when choosing an exchange platform for their transactions.

Lastly, it is important to note that liquidity protocols also play a crucial role in the cryptocurrency market. Liquidity protocols enable investors to buy and sell digital assets at more advantageous prices by aggregating buy and sell orders from different exchange platforms. Liquidity protocols improve market liquidity and reduce price discrepancies between different exchange platforms.

Stablecoins and Lending Mechanisms

In the world of cryptocurrencies, stablecoins are digital currencies designed to maintain a stable value, often linked to an underlying asset or fiat currency such as the US dollar or the euro. They allow users to protect themselves against the volatility often associated with other cryptocurrencies like Bitcoin or Ethereum.

The mechanism behind stablecoins is simple: for every unit of stablecoin issued, an equivalent amount of the underlying asset is held in reserve. Hence, when a user buys or sells a stablecoin, the price is adjusted accordingly to maintain its stable value. Stablecoins can be traded on trading platforms and used as a means of payment.

In addition to stability, stablecoins also offer advantages in terms of lending. Users can use their stablecoins as collateral to obtain loans in cryptocurrencies or fiat currency. Cryptocurrency lending platforms also allow users to lend their stablecoins to other users in exchange for an interest rate. These loans can be used for investments or everyday expenses.

A popular example of a stablecoin is Tether (USDT), which is tied to the US dollar. Other stablecoins include USD Coin (USDC), Dai (DAI), and Binance USD (BUSD). Each of these stablecoins is backed by a reserve of US dollars, ensuring stability.

However, it is important to note that stablecoins can also present risks, particularly in terms of regulation and trust in underlying reserves. Therefore, it is crucial to choose stablecoins issued by trusted entities and monitor their evaluation regularly.

DAOs and Decentralized Governance

Decentralized Autonomous Organizations (DAOs) are organizations without a central legal entity that operate based on predefined rules executed automatically by a system of smart contracts. These organizations are built on blockchain technology, providing increased transparency, security, and resilience. DAOs allow their members to make decisions democratically and in a decentralized manner, using token-based voting systems.

Decentralized governance, which is one of the fundamental principles of DAOs, offers an interesting alternative to traditional centralized governance models. It allows for greater transparency, fair distribution of power, and better member participation. DAOs can be used for a variety of projects, such as crowdfunding, fund management, governance of open-source projects, or even management of online communities.

DAOs have seen significant growth in recent years, particularly in the cryptocurrency and DeFi ecosystem. Many DeFi platforms and protocols are based on DAOs, and members can make decisions regarding rules, protocols, improvements, and updates. DAOs are often used for the governance of liquidity protocols, which are at the heart of the DeFi ecosystem.

However, decentralized governance does not always guarantee optimal or fair decisions. Issues such as lack of participation, vote manipulation, centralization of power, or corruption can occur, just as in centralized governance models. Therefore, it is important to have appropriate security and monitoring mechanisms to ensure fair and transparent governance.

Risks and Challenges of DeFi

Decentralized Finance (DeFi) has experienced rapid growth in recent years, attracting billions of dollars in investment and offering attractive returns to investors. However, despite the advantages it offers, DeFi also carries significant risks and challenges that must be taken into account.

The first risk associated with DeFi is security. As all transactions are conducted on public blockchains, malicious actors may seek to exploit vulnerabilities in smart contracts or exchange platforms to steal funds. Additionally, human errors or bugs in the code can lead to significant losses for investors.

The second risk is liquidity. Assets held in smart contracts may be difficult to exchange for other assets or withdraw as cash. This can result in significant losses for investors who need liquidity quickly.

The third risk is volatility. Cryptocurrencies and tokens used in DeFi can experience significant fluctuations in value in a short period, which can result in significant losses for investors.

Furthermore, DeFi presents significant regulatory challenges. Regulators around the world are closely scrutinizing DeFi-related activities and seeking to establish a clear regulatory framework to protect investors and prevent criminal activities.

Lastly, DeFi faces significant governance challenges. DeFi platforms are often governed by communities of token holders who vote on important decisions. However, these governance systems are often opaque and lack transparency, which can result in decisions made in the interest of a few individuals to the detriment of the broader community.

Despite these risks and challenges, DeFi offers many potential benefits for investors. It enables fast, low-cost, and accessible financial transactions without the need for intermediaries. It also offers attractive returns to investors through innovative lending and staking mechanisms.

NFTs and the Digital Economy

Non-Fungible Tokens (NFTs) are a recent innovation in the cryptocurrency world that has captivated global attention. NFTs are unique digital assets that represent ownership of a digital object, whether it be a piece of art, a video, music, or even a tweet. Unlike traditional cryptocurrencies like Bitcoin or Ethereum, NFTs are not interchangeable, and each NFT is unique.

NFTs have revolutionized the digital economy by offering content creators a new way to monetize their work. Creators can sell NFTs representing their digital artwork, allowing them to benefit from the rarity and value of their creation. For example, in March 2021, digital artist Beeple sold a digital artwork as an NFT for a record-breaking $69 million.

NFTs are also a means for fans to support their favorite artists while owning a unique and authentic object. Fans can acquire a piece of their favorite artist's history while contributing to their financial success.

However, NFTs have also faced criticism due to their environmental impact. Most NFTs are created and traded on the Ethereum blockchain, which consumes a significant amount of energy to secure its network. This environmental issue must be taken into account when using NFTs, and solutions need to be found to reduce their carbon footprint.

Non-Fungible Tokens (NFTs) and the Digital Economy

The Principles and Applications of NFTs

Non-Fungible Tokens (NFTs) are unique digital assets that represent ownership and authenticity of a specific digital object, such as artwork, a video, a tweet, or even a gaming token. NFTs are created on the blockchain, which means their ownership and authenticity can be publicly and securely verified.

NFTs have experienced explosive growth in recent years, with record-breaking sales of digital artwork and gaming tokens. NFTs provide a new opportunity for artists, creators, and game developers to monetize unique digital objects directly to their fans, without the need for intermediaries such as auction houses or game distribution platforms.

NFTs can also hold sentimental and symbolic value for their owners, serving as markers of their participation or support for a specific community or cause. NFTs can be used to create voting tokens for community members or to reward contributors to an open-source project.

However, NFTs can also be used for fraudulent or illegal activities, such as counterfeiting, selling stolen goods, or money laundering. Regulators and government authorities are seeking to better understand the implications of NFTs for financial security and consumer protection, and to develop policies and regulations to mitigate the associated risks.

NFT Exchange and Creation Platforms

NFT exchange and creation platforms have taken the digital art and unique collectibles industry by storm. NFTs, or non-fungible tokens, are digital assets that represent ownership of digital objects such as images, videos, music, and more. NFT exchange platforms allow artists and creators to sell their digital works as NFTs, while NFT creation platforms offer the ability to create and customize NFTs based on users' needs and preferences.

The most popular NFT exchange platforms include OpenSea, Rarible, SuperRare, and Nifty Gateway. These platforms enable users to safely and seamlessly buy, sell, and collect NFTs. Artists can also use these platforms to sell their digital creations as NFTs and receive fair compensation for their work.

NFT creation platforms are also gaining popularity, offering users the ability to create and customize NFTs according to their own specifications. Well-known NFT creation platforms include Mintable, NiftyKit, and OpenSea's Creator. These platforms allow users to create unique NFTs from their own images, videos, or music and customize each NFT by including specific elements such as attributes or special properties.

NFTs have become a new form of collecting unique and valuable items. NFT exchange and creation platforms provide artists and creators with a new opportunity to sell their work and make it known to a wider audience. Collectors can also take advantage of these platforms to acquire unique and rare digital artworks securely and transparently through blockchain technology.

The Economic and Cultural Aspects of NFTs

Non-Fungible Tokens (NFTs) are a recent technological innovation in the world of cryptocurrencies. NFTs enable the digital representation of unique assets, such as artwork, video game tokens, or even tweets, using blockchain technology. NFTs have become a significant topic of discussion in economic and cultural circles due to their potential impact on the art, entertainment, and cultural industries.

From an economic perspective, NFTs offer new opportunities for artists and content creators to sell unique digital assets and earn income from their work. NFTs also provide proof of authenticity and ownership for digital assets, which is particularly important for the art and culture industries that have traditionally struggled with counterfeiting and piracy.

However, NFTs have also raised concerns regarding their impact on the art and culture industry. Some fear that NFTs may become a new form of financial speculation and speculative bubble rather than a true advancement for artists and content creators. Therefore, it is important to understand the mechanics of NFTs and ensure that their use is responsible and sustainable.

From a cultural perspective, NFTs also offer new perspectives for content creation and dissemination. Artists and content creators can leverage the possibilities offered by blockchain technology to experiment with new modes of creation and content sharing. NFTs also break down traditional barriers between art and technology, paving the way for new forms of creativity and expression.

However, NFTs have also raised questions about access and cultural diversity. Some fear that NFTs may only be accessible to a limited audience of wealthy collectors, which could limit cultural and creative diversity. Therefore, it is important to ensure that the use of NFTs remains accessible and open to all in order to promote a more inclusive and diverse culture.

Investment and Portfolio Management

Investment Strategies and Associated Risks

Cryptocurrencies have become a highly popular investment subject in recent years, with many investors seeking to profit from the rapid growth of this expanding market. However, it is important to note that investing in cryptocurrencies also comes with considerable risks, primarily due to the volatile nature of this market.

One of the most common investment strategies in cryptocurrencies is to adopt a «buy and hold» approach, which involves buying a cryptocurrency at a given price and holding it for an extended period in the hope that its value will increase in the long term. This strategy can be effective for investors who believe in the long-term viability of a particular cryptocurrency, but it also comes with significant risks due to market volatility and price fluctuations.

Another common investment strategy in cryptocurrencies is day trading, which involves buying and selling cryptocurrencies on a daily or weekly basis to make quick profits by exploiting price fluctuations. While this approach can be profitable for experienced investors, it is also highly risky due to market volatility and the need for in-depth knowledge of technical analysis to make effective trading decisions.

It is also important to note that investing in cryptocurrencies is subject to considerable regulatory risks, as many countries are seeking to regulate or even completely ban cryptocurrencies due to security and fraud concerns. Investors must be aware of these risks and closely monitor regulatory developments in the countries where they invest.

Fundamental Analysis and Technical Analysis Tools

When it comes to investing in cryptocurrencies, it is crucial to consider several factors to assess the value of a digital currency and its future performance. Fundamental analysis is an approach that involves examining the underlying economic and financial aspects of a cryptocurrency, such as its adoption, usage, technology, and partnerships. This analysis can help investors determine if a cryptocurrency has long-term growth potential.

One key aspect of fundamental analysis is examining the adoption and usage of the cryptocurrency. Factors that can affect the adoption and usage of a cryptocurrency include ease of use, security, partnerships with established companies, and merchant acceptance. For example, Tesla's adoption of Bitcoin has been a significant factor in the cryptocurrency's value increase in 2021.

Furthermore, fundamental analysis can also focus on the underlying technology of the cryptocurrency. Investors can evaluate the quality and efficiency of the blockchain technology, as well as how it is implemented in the cryptocurrency. The analysis may also look at recent or future technological innovations that could enhance the security, speed, or functionality of the cryptocurrency.

In addition to fundamental analysis, technical analysis can also be used to evaluate market trends and price movements of a cryptocurrency. Technical analysis involves examining price charts, volume trends, and other technical indicators to determine past and predict future trends. However, it is important to remember that technical analysis does not take into account the fundamental factors that can influence the price of a cryptocurrency.

It is important to emphasize that fundamental and technical analysis do not guarantee success in cryptocurrency investments. Investments in cryptocurrencies are highly speculative and can be subject to significant volatility. Investors must consider multiple factors, including their own risk tolerance, before deciding to invest in cryptocurrencies.

Diversification and Portfolio Management

Diversification and portfolio management are crucial concepts for cryptocurrency investors. As with any type of investment, it is important to diversify one's portfolio to reduce risks and maximize potential gains. Diversification involves spreading risks across different assets, categories, and behaviors.

It is important to note that diversification does not guarantee gains, but it helps minimize potential losses if an asset or market category performs poorly. Diversification can be achieved by investing in different cryptocurrencies, different categories of cryptocurrencies, or in different sectors of the economy related to cryptocurrencies.

Portfolio management is also crucial for cryptocurrency investors. It is important to have a clear and well-defined portfolio management strategy to make informed decisions on asset acquisition, sale, or retention. This strategy should include clear objectives, asset allocation, profit and loss thresholds, and regular monitoring of market developments.

It is important to understand that the cryptocurrency market is extremely volatile and can be influenced by unforeseen external factors. Cryptocurrency investors must be prepared to accept potential losses and exercise patience for their portfolio to generate long-term returns.

It is also important to note that cryptocurrency portfolio management requires in-depth knowledge of different cryptocurrencies, market trends, and economic factors that can influence the market. Investors must regularly follow news and technological developments in the cryptocurrency universe to make informed decisions on portfolio management.

Taxation and Regulation

Taxation and regulation of cryptocurrencies are crucial subjects for any investor or user of these digital assets. While cryptocurrencies are often associated with decentralization and financial freedom, they are also subject to tax and regulatory rules in many countries.

In terms of taxation, cryptocurrencies are often treated as financial assets, which means that gains made on these assets may be subject to income tax or capital gains tax. However, tax rules vary from one country to another, so it is important to research the applicable rules in one's jurisdiction. Additionally, it is important to note that cryptocurrency transactions can also be subject to value-added tax (VAT) or similar taxes in certain countries.

Regarding regulation, many countries have implemented regulatory frameworks to oversee cryptocurrency transactions. This may include compliance requirements for anti-money laundering (AML) and counter-terrorism financing (CTF), registration or licensing requirements for cryptocurrency exchanges, or restrictions on investments in these digital assets.

It is important to note that these regulations can evolve rapidly, and cryptocurrency investors and users must stay informed about the latest developments. For example, some countries have recently taken measures to ban or restrict the use of certain cryptocurrencies or tighten regulations on cryptocurrency exchanges.

In conclusion, taxation and regulation of cryptocurrencies are complex and constantly evolving subjects. It is therefore essential to research the applicable rules in one's jurisdiction and stay informed about the latest regulatory developments. Any cryptocurrency investor or user must be aware of the potential risks associated with these digital assets and take measures to limit these risks as much as possible.

New Forms of Financing and Investment

Initial Coin Offerings (ICO) and Security Token Offerings (STO)

Initial Coin Offerings (ICO) and Security Token Offerings (STO) are popular methods of financing for projects based on blockchain technology. ICOs and STOs allow investors to acquire tokens or securities that represent a stake in the respective project. ICOs and STOs have the potential to revolutionize the world of finance by offering new investment opportunities for individuals and businesses.

ICOs were first introduced in 2013 with the creation of Mastercoin, which was the first successful ICO in history. Since then, thousands of projects have used this method to raise funds. ICOs are often used by startups to finance the development of new projects based on blockchain technology. Investors purchase cryptocurrency tokens issued by the project in exchange for funds. These tokens can be used to access services or products offered by the project or can be traded on cryptocurrency exchange platforms.

STOs, on the other hand, are offerings of secure and regulated securities issued on the blockchain. Unlike ICOs, STOs are subject to strict regulations regarding security and investor protection, making them a safer and more reliable financing option. STOs can be used to raise funds for larger projects such as real estate, investment funds, or infrastructure projects.

ICOs and STOs offer unique advantages for investors and issuers. They provide funding opportunities for early-stage projects that struggle to obtain traditional financing. Investors can acquire a stake in the project in exchange for their funds, which can be profitable if the project is successful.

However, there are risks associated with ICOs and STOs, and investors must exercise caution when investing in these projects. ICOs can be susceptible to fraud, and investors may lose their money if the project fails. STOs are also subject to regulatory risks, and investors must ensure that issuers comply with applicable laws and regulations.

Crowdfunding and Lending Platforms

Crowdfunding and lending platforms have emerged as a means of financing cryptocurrency-related projects. They offer an alternative to traditional lenders by allowing individuals and businesses to borrow directly from the cryptocurrency investor community.

Crowdfunding and lending platforms are typically decentralized platforms that operate on the blockchain and use smart contracts to automate transactions between lenders and borrowers. Lenders can lend funds in exchange for an interest rate, and borrowers can access funding without going through traditional financial institutions.

These platforms also allow investors to diversify their

portfolios by investing in a variety of cryptocurrency-related projects, such as mining projects, infrastructure projects, software development projects, ICOs, and other innovative projects.

However, it should be noted that these platforms are often associated with high risks. Borrowers may be unregulated individuals or businesses, and projects can be highly speculative. Therefore, investors must exercise caution when investing in cryptocurrency-related crowdfunding or lending projects.

There are several blockchain-based crowdfunding and lending platforms, such as EthLend, SALT, Celsius Network, Nexo, BlockFi, Bitbond, and many others. These platforms offer various services and different advantages, so it is important to conduct thorough research before choosing a platform to use.

Investment Funds and Crypto Assets

Crypto assets have attracted the attention of institutional investors in recent years, and many investment funds have been created to enable investors to participate in this growing market. Investment funds offer investors exposure to crypto assets through a traditional fund structure, which allows for professional management and risk diversification.

Crypto asset investment funds can take different forms. Funds can be passive, replicating the performance of a crypto asset market index, or active, seeking to outperform the market index through active management.

Passive funds are usually index funds or exchange-traded funds (ETFs) designed to track the performance of a crypto asset market index, such as Bitcoin or Ethereum. These funds are designed to provide direct exposure to the crypto asset market without requiring in-depth knowledge of the underlying technology or markets.

Active funds, on the other hand, are managed by investment professionals who seek to outperform the market index by investing in a selection of crypto assets. These funds are designed to provide exposure to the crypto asset market while offering professional management and risk diversification.

Crypto asset investment funds are subject to strict regulation in many countries, and potential investors must ensure that the funds they are interested in are regulated and compliant with applicable standards.

It is important to note that crypto assets are a constantly evolving market with considerable risks and opportunities. Investors must be aware of these risks and exercise caution when investing in crypto asset investment funds.

Cryptocurrencies and the Global Economy

Impacts on Banks and Financial Institutions

Cryptocurrencies have a major impact on banks and financial institutions. They have become aware of the potential of cryptocurrencies and are increasingly involved in their development and adoption.

Banks face several challenges regarding cryptocurrencies. First, they must adapt to the emergence of new payment and fund transfer methods, which could threaten their traditional business model. Cryptocurrencies offer faster, more secure, and less costly solutions than traditional financial transactions. As a result, banks must be able to meet the needs of customers who wish to use cryptocurrencies for their financial transactions.

Second, banks must be aware of the risks associated with cryptocurrencies, such as price volatility, transaction security, and fraud risks. To do so, banks must develop security and monitoring solutions to protect their clients from cyberattacks.

Financial institutions are also concerned about cryptocurrencies. Institutional investors have started investing in cryptocurrencies and digital assets, leading to an increase in the market capitalization of these assets. Consequently, financial institutions have begun exploring new investment opportunities in cryptocurrencies and developing financial products based on these assets.

However, financial regulators have started expressing concerns about the risks associated with cryptocurrencies and have begun strengthening their oversight of cryptocurrency exchanges. Financial institutions must therefore be able to comply with constantly evolving regulations.

Finally, banks and financial institutions must also adapt to the emergence of decentralized finance (DeFi) based on cryptocurrencies. DeFi offers decentralized financial services, such as lending, exchanges, and smart contracts, without the need for a third party to manage them. Banks must therefore be able to position themselves in this emerging ecosystem and find ways to collaborate with DeFi protocols.

The Adoption of Cryptocurrencies by Businesses and Merchants

The adoption of cryptocurrencies by businesses and merchants is a rapidly expanding field. Indeed, an increasing number of companies choose to accept payments in cryptocurrencies, especially Bitcoin and Ethereum. This adoption is due to several reasons, including the growing popularity of cryptocurrencies and their increasing use as a means of payment by consumers.

The adoption of cryptocurrencies by businesses can also be motivated by financial advantages. Indeed, cryptocurrency payments are often cheaper than traditional payments, as there is no need to go through costly financial intermediaries such as banks. Additionally, cryptocurrency payments are generally faster and more secure than traditional payments, as transactions are made directly between parties without intermediaries.

However, the adoption of cryptocurrencies by businesses is not without challenges. Firstly, cryptocurrencies are still relatively new and unfamiliar, which can make their adoption difficult for some companies. Moreover, cryptocurrencies are subject to significant volatility, which can make cryptocurrency transactions risky for businesses.

Despite these challenges, many companies adopt cryptocurrencies as a means of payment, and some merchants even offer discounts to customers who pay with cryptocurrencies. Major companies such as Microsoft, Tesla, and PayPal already accept Bitcoin payments, and it is expected that others will follow their example in the future.

Cryptocurrencies as a Store of Value and Means of Payment

Cryptocurrencies, especially Bitcoin, were initially designed as a decentralized and autonomous alternative to the traditional financial system. Since then, they have evolved to become a store of value and means of payment used by millions of people worldwide. Cryptocurrencies offer several advantages as a store of value and means of payment, including security, speed, and ease of use.

As a store of value, cryptocurrencies have unique characteristics that differentiate them from traditional currencies. Firstly, they are decentralized, which means they are not controlled by a single entity or financial institution. Additionally, their supply is limited, which means they are relatively immune to inflation. Finally, cryptocurrencies are often used to diversify investment portfolios, as they are not correlated with traditional financial markets.

As a means of payment, cryptocurrencies offer practical advantages compared to traditional payment methods. Firstly, transactions are quick and efficient. Additionally, transaction fees are generally lower than those charged by banks and other financial institutions. Finally, transactions are often anonymous, which can provide users with an extra level of privacy.

However, cryptocurrencies also have limitations as a store of value and means of payment. Firstly, their volatility can make their use as a store of value uncertain. Additionally, their adoption as a means of payment is limited by the availability of merchants accepting cryptocurrencies. Finally, the anonymity that is often considered an advantage can also facilitate illegal activities such as money laundering and terrorist financing.

In conclusion, cryptocurrencies can be an interesting means to diversify investment portfolios and provide an alternative to traditional payment methods. However, it is important to understand their advantages and limitations before using them as a store of value or means of payment.

The Social and Geopolitical Implications of Cryptocurrencies

The Democratization of Access to Financial Services

One of the key objectives of cryptocurrencies is to democratize access to financial services. Indeed, cryptocurrencies enable individuals, businesses, and even states that were previously excluded from the traditional financial system to benefit from access to banking and financial services.

Cryptocurrencies were born out of the desire to create a fairer and more equitable financial system, free from the inequalities and discriminations inherent to the traditional financial system. They allow bypassing the barriers to entry in the traditional financial system, such as solvency requirements, high costs, or geographical constraints.

With cryptocurrencies, anyone can have access to a bank account and conduct financial transactions at a low cost, without requiring prior authorization and without being subjected to the restrictions imposed by banks or governments.

Indeed, cryptocurrencies are often decentralized and based on blockchain technology, which means that they are managed by a network of peers rather than a central entity. Transactions are validated through consensus within this network, which allows for greater transparency and trust in the system.

Furthermore, cryptocurrencies are often associated with microcredit and financial inclusion projects in developing countries, where traditional banking services are often inaccessible or costly. Cryptocurrencies can offer affordable and secure payment solutions, allowing these populations to escape financial precariousness.

However, it should be noted that cryptocurrencies are not yet widely used as a means of payment, partly due to the volatility of their value. But many projects are underway to develop stable cryptocurrencies, indexed to fiat currencies, to overcome this issue.

Cryptocurrencies and Privacy Protection

Cryptocurrencies were created to provide an alternative to traditional financial systems, offering increased security and enhanced privacy to users. However, this privacy can be called into question, particularly with regard to privacy protection.

Most cryptocurrencies are not completely anonymous, as all transactions are recorded in the blockchain, a decentralized public ledger. Wallet addresses are also public, which means that transactions can be tracked and analyzed.

However, there are cryptocurrencies that offer enhanced privacy protection through technologies such as coin mixing (CoinJoin) or hidden addresses (RingCT). These cryptocurrencies are often referred to as «privacy coins» and include projects like Monero, Zcash, and Dash.

Unfortunately, these cryptocurrencies are often used for illicit activities such as money laundering and terrorism financing. Financial regulators worldwide are therefore working to implement regulations to combat these practices.

Moreover, it is important to note that centralized cryptocurrency exchanges, which allow the buying and selling of cryptocurrencies, can also compromise users' privacy. These exchanges must comply with anti-money laundering and fraud laws, which often require them to collect personal information from their users, such as identification documents and bank statements.

To preserve the privacy of cryptocurrency users, it is important to choose privacy-respecting exchange platforms and to prefer privacy-focused cryptocurrencies. Users can also use offline cryptocurrency wallets or hardware wallets for increased security.

Regulatory Challenges and Conflicts of Interest

Regulatory challenges and conflicts of interest represent a major issue for the cryptocurrency market. Indeed, the decentralized and unregulated nature of cryptocurrencies poses legal and ethical problems, particularly concerning money laundering, terrorism financing, and consumer protection.

On one hand, regulatory authorities seek to protect investors and consumers by establishing standards and regulations for cryptocurrency transactions. On the other hand, cryptocurrency advocates oppose any form of regulation that could limit freedom and transactional anonymity.

Conflicts of interest can also arise when influential market players, such as exchange platforms, miners, and developers, have personal interests that do not align with those of the users. For example, an exchange platform could manipulate prices to increase its own profits, or a developer could create a new cryptocurrency purely for quick enrichment.

Faced with these challenges, governments and regulatory authorities are trying to find a balance between the need to protect consumers and prevent illegal activities, and the respect for the principles of decentralization and freedom of expression that underlie cryptocurrencies.

Many jurisdictions have adopted a pragmatic approach by recognizing cryptocurrencies as financial assets and implementing rules for cryptocurrency transactions. However, others have banned or strictly regulated cryptocurrencies, which can limit their adoption and use.

It is important for cryptocurrency investors and users to be aware of these regulatory challenges and conflicts of interest in order to make informed decisions and protect their investments. Responsible transparency and regulation can help strengthen trust in the cryptocurrency market and promote their future adoption.

Cryptocurrencies as Monetary Policy Instruments

Cryptocurrencies have an interesting potential as instruments for monetary policy. Unlike traditional currencies that are issued by central banks under government control, cryptocurrencies are issued in a decentralized manner and their supply is regulated by mathematical algorithms. This means that they can offer benefits such as transparency, security, and efficiency while avoiding government monetary policies that are often subject to political and economic influences.

The use of cryptocurrencies as monetary policy instruments can be considered in several ways. Firstly, cryptocurrencies can be used as an alternative to traditional currencies, providing individuals and businesses with an alternative to government-regulated fiat currencies. Additionally, governments can use cryptocurrencies as a means of regulating the economy by algorithmically adjusting supply and demand.

For example, a government could issue a regulated cryptocurrency in limited quantity, which would be used to regulate the economy's supply and demand. If the economy starts to slow down, the government could increase the supply of cryptocurrency to encourage growth. Conversely, if the economy becomes overheated and inflation starts to rise, the government could reduce the supply of cryptocurrency to curb growth.

Of course, the use of cryptocurrencies as monetary policy

instruments is not without risk. The supply and demand of cryptocurrencies can be influenced by external factors such as speculation, market manipulation, and global events. Furthermore, the use of cryptocurrencies can be difficult to regulate, which can lead to security and fraud issues.

Nevertheless, with adequate regulation efforts and responsible management, the use of cryptocurrencies as monetary policy instruments could offer significant benefits. Cryptocurrencies could provide increased transparency, operational efficiency, cost reduction, and resilience to economic shocks, while offering an alternative to government-regulated currencies.

The Environmental Impact of Cryptocurrencies

The Energy Consumption of Cryptocurrencies

The energy consumed by cryptocurrencies is becoming an increasingly concerning issue for the environment. Indeed, mining cryptocurrencies like Bitcoin require a massive amount of energy due to the transaction validation process that utilizes a significant amount of computing power. According to certain estimates, the annual energy consumption of the Bitcoin network is equivalent to that of a small country like Argentina.

This high energy consumption is primarily due to the proof-of-work (PoW) mechanism employed by Bitcoin and other similar cryptocurrencies. In the case of Bitcoin, the transaction validation process involves solving complex mathematical puzzles to create a new block of transactions. To achieve this, miners must perform intensive calculations using powerful computers that consume a significant amount of electricity.

However, it is important to note that energy consumption varies considerably depending on the specific cryptocurrency and its validation method. Cryptocurrencies that utilize alternative consensus mechanisms such as proof-of-stake (PoS) generally consume less energy than those using proof-of-work.

It is also important to highlight that cryptocurrency miners are increasingly seeking to utilize renewable energy sources to reduce their carbon footprint. Initiatives such as the Bitcoin Mining Council have been established to encourage the use of renewable energy in cryptocurrency mining.

Lastly, it is essential to understand that the energy consumption of cryptocurrencies must be placed in perspective compared to other sectors of the global economy. While Bitcoin's energy consumption is high, it is still significantly lower than that of the traditional banking and gold industries. Therefore, it is important not to demonize cryptocurrencies as a whole, but rather to seek solutions to reduce their environmental impact while acknowledging their economic and technological potential.

Solutions for Greener Mining

Cryptocurrency mining often faces criticism for its environmental impact. Indeed, mining certain cryptocurrencies, such as Bitcoin, requires a significant amount of electricity and therefore emits a large quantity of greenhouse gases. However, there are solutions to make cryptocurrency mining more environmentally friendly.

Firstly, renewable energies can be used to power cryptocurrency mining farms. Renewable energy sources like solar, wind, or hydroelectric power are increasingly accessible and offer a more sustainable alternative to fossil fuels. Cryptocurrency mining companies can therefore invest in facilities that utilize these energy sources to reduce their environmental impact.

Another solution is to improve the energy efficiency of mining equipment. Companies can utilize more efficient equipment to reduce the amount of electricity required for mining. Mining equipment manufacturers can also design more eco-friendly products by utilizing components that consume less energy and optimizing cooling processes.

Finally, a solution to reduce the environmental impact of cryptocurrency mining is to transition to more sustainable consensus protocols. Proof-of-work consensus protocols, used by Bitcoin, are highly energy-intensive. Proof-of-stake protocols, used by cryptocurrencies like Ethereum, consume much less energy and are, therefore, more eco-friendly. Other protocols such as proof-of-participation, proof-of-authority, and proof-of-capacity are also more sustainable alternatives.

Initiatives for a Sustainable Blockchain

Environmental concerns have become a hot topic in the cryptocurrency field. The energy consumption required for mining and validating transactions on the blockchain is constantly increasing, raising concerns about its environmental impact.

However, numerous initiatives are underway to make the blockchain more sustainable and environmentally friendly.

One such initiative is to encourage the use of renewable energy for cryptocurrency mining. Miners currently predominantly use electricity generated from fossil fuels, resulting in greenhouse gas emissions. By transitioning to solar, wind, or hydroelectric power, miners could significantly reduce their carbon footprint.

Additionally, alternative consensus protocols are also a solution to reducing cryptocurrency energy consumption. For instance, proof-of-stake is a consensus method that does not require mining and, therefore, is much more energy-efficient than proof-of-work.

Low-energy blockchains are also emerging, particularly in the realm of payment transactions. For example, the cryptocurrency Nano utilizes a consensus protocol called Open Representative Voting (ORV) that does not require competition of intensive and energy-consuming calculations.

Lastly, there is also an initiative to utilize the heat generated by cryptocurrency mining for other purposes. Cryptocurrency data centers can produce a significant amount of heat that could be recovered and used to heat buildings or for industrial processes, thereby reducing energy consumption and greenhouse gas emissions.

Trends and Future of Cryptocurrencies

Upcoming Technological Innovations

There are numerous fascinating technological innovations on the horizon in the field of cryptocurrencies. New advancements are being developed to enhance the performance of existing blockchain networks, improve transaction security and privacy, and expand the use cases of cryptocurrencies into new sectors.

One of the most promising advancements is the adoption of smart contract technology, which allows the creation of executable programs on the blockchain. Smart contracts enable the implementation of automated contracts between parties without the need for a trusted third party, such as a notary or lawyer. This technology could have practical applications in areas such as insurance, finance, real estate, and human resources.

Another major innovation is the use of Proof of Stake (PoS) to validate transactions on the blockchain. Unlike Proof of Work, which is used by Bitcoin and other cryptocurrencies and requires enormous amounts of energy to solve complex mathematical problems and validate transactions, Proof of Stake does not. This could significantly reduce the environmental footprint of cryptocurrencies and improve network performance.

Transaction privacy is also an active research area in the cryptocurrency world. Cryptocurrencies like Monero and Zcash already utilize advanced cryptographic algorithms to mask users' identities and make transactions anonymous. Further improvements could allow users to have even finer control over the privacy of their transactions without compromising network security.

Lastly, interoperability between different blockchains is another key technological advancement for the development of cryptocurrencies. Currently, each blockchain operates autonomously and cannot easily communicate with other blockchains. Projects such as Cosmos and Polkadot aim to create bridges between different blockchains, enabling users to exchange cryptocurrencies and assets across different chains.

Evolution of the Regulatory Landscape

The evolution of the regulatory landscape for cryptocurrencies has been one of the most significant issues in recent years. Governments worldwide have sought to better understand cryptocurrencies and regulate their use.

In some countries, regulations have been relatively relaxed, while in others, they have been more restrictive. Generally, governments have aimed to strike a balance between investor protection and promoting innovation.

In the United States, the Securities and Exchange Commission (SEC) has played a key role in cryptocurrency regulation. In 2019, the SEC issued guidelines detailing how companies should treat digital tokens. Companies must now prove that their tokens are assets and not securities, otherwise they must comply with applicable securities rules.

In Europe, the situation is more complex as each European Union member country has its own regulations. However, the European Commission proposed a European regulatory framework for crypto-assets in September 2020, which includes transparency requirements, investor protection, and anti-money laundering measures.

In Asia, the regulatory landscape is also complex. China banned Initial Coin Offerings (ICOs) in 2017 and continued to ban the entire cryptocurrency industry in 2021. Japan, on the other hand, has adopted strict regulations to govern cryptocurrency exchanges.

Overall, the regulatory landscape for cryptocurrencies is constantly evolving. Governments are seeking to find a balance between promoting innovation and investor protection. Investors and cryptocurrency users must be aware of the applicable regulatory rules in their countries and comply with them.

Adoption of Cryptocurrencies by Institutions and Businesses

The adoption of cryptocurrencies by institutions and businesses is an ever-evolving phenomenon. Since the early days of Bitcoin, many companies have become interested in cryptocurrencies and the underlying blockchain technology. This has led to a wide range of applications, from simply holding cryptocurrencies to using blockchain to enhance the efficiency of business processes.

Major financial institutions have also begun integrating cryptocurrencies into their operations. Investment banks, for example, have started offering cryptocurrency trading services to their institutional clients. Some companies have even begun accepting cryptocurrency payments from their customers.

The adoption of cryptocurrencies by businesses has been facilitated by several factors. Firstly, blockchain technology offers a high level of security and transparency, which can be particularly important for financial transactions. Additionally, cryptocurrencies can offer cost benefits by reducing transaction fees and payment processing costs.

Cryptocurrencies can also help businesses expand their customer base by providing an alternative payment option for those without a bank account or credit card. They can facilitate international transactions by avoiding exchange fees and speeding up fund transfers.

However, the adoption of cryptocurrencies by businesses can also present challenges. Significant value fluctuations of cryptocurrencies can make transactions unstable and unpredictable. Companies must also be aware of the risks associated with holding cryptocurrencies, including the risk of theft and hacking.

Despite these challenges, the adoption of cryptocurrencies by institutions and businesses is steadily increasing. Companies looking to modernize and remain competitive must be aware of this trend and explore the opportunities offered by blockchain technology and cryptocurrencies.

Market Outlook

Cryptocurrencies have experienced phenomenal growth since their creation, and their popularity continues to soar. The market outlook for cryptocurrencies is promising and offers numerous opportunities for investors, businesses, and individuals.

Firstly, the adoption of cryptocurrencies by financial institutions and businesses is expected to continue in the coming years. More and more companies are integrating cryptocurrencies into their business models by accepting cryptocurrency payments or investing in digital assets. Major banks and financial institutions have also started exploring opportunities offered by cryptocurrencies by offering trading and custody services.

Secondly, improved regulation is expected to enhance the legitimacy of cryptocurrencies and attract a larger number of institutional investors. Regulatory authorities worldwide are working to establish clear regulatory frameworks for cryptocurrencies, which should help investors feel more secure and understand the risks associated with cryptocurrencies.

Furthermore, the underlying technology of cryptocurrencies, blockchain, continues to develop and improve. Enhancements to blockchain technology will address some of the current issues with cryptocurrencies, such as scalability and security. Research projects are also underway to develop faster and more efficient blockchains, as well as stronger consensus protocols.

Lastly, decentralized finance (DeFi) is a growing trend in the cryptocurrency ecosystem. DeFi allows users to participate in decentralized financial services such as lending and trading without the need for intermediaries. DeFi is transforming the financial sector and is expected to continue growing in the years to come.

Conclusion and Recommendations

Key Takeaways

There are many key takeaways to consider regarding cryptocurrencies. Firstly, it is important to understand that cryptocurrencies are a revolutionary technology that has the potential to change the way we conduct financial transactions. The blockchain technology, on which cryptocurrencies are based, allows for decentralized and transparent transaction management, providing an alternative to trust-based intermediaries such as banks.

When it comes to different cryptocurrencies, it is essential to understand the specificities of each one, as they may have different objectives, security protocols, and levels of volatility. For example, Bitcoin is often seen as a digital store of value, whereas Ethereum is the leading development platform for decentralized applications.

Security is also a key element in cryptocurrencies, as they are often targeted by cyber attacks. Therefore, it is important to understand different security mechanisms such as cryptography, consensus protocols, and secure wallets.

Investors must also be aware of the risks associated with cryptocurrency investments, such as price volatility and regulatory risks. Having a good understanding of investment strategies, fundamental and technical analysis, as well as portfolio management, is essential.

Finally, cryptocurrencies have the potential to impact the global economy and social and geopolitical issues. For example, they could potentially offer more equitable access to financial services in developing countries, but they could also lead to conflicts of interest and regulatory challenges.

Best Practices for Navigating the Cryptocurrency Universe

To navigate the cryptocurrency universe, it is important to follow certain best practices. First and foremost, it is essential to stay informed about the latest news and market trends by regularly consulting reliable and diverse sources such as specialized blogs, community forums, academic publications, and research reports.

Next, it is recommended to familiarize oneself with the fundamental principles of blockchain technology, as well as the consensus mechanisms and security protocols associated with different cryptocurrencies. This will provide a better understanding of the risks and benefits related to investing and portfolio management.

It is also important to carefully choose cryptocurrency exchange platforms and storage services, prioritizing those with proven track records in terms of security and reliability. It is recommended not to store all cryptocurrencies on a single platform or electronic wallet, but rather to distribute them across multiple different addresses.

In terms of portfolio management, it is advisable to adopt a long-term investment strategy, diversifying one's portfolio based on individual goals and risk profile. It is also recommended not to invest more than one can afford to lose and to avoid panicking during market fluctuations.

Finally, it is important to comply with local regulations concerning cryptocurrencies and to report any gains or losses to the relevant tax authorities. It is also recommended to be aware of fraud and scams risks and to never disclose private keys or personal information to untrustworthy third parties.

Future Perspectives for Cryptocurrencies

The future outlook for cryptocurrencies is highly promising. Technological advancements in the blockchain field, as well as the increasing adoption of cryptocurrencies by businesses and individuals, are paving the way for numerous opportunities and continued market growth.

Firstly, cryptocurrencies will continue to evolve and diversify. New cryptocurrencies will emerge, offering specific features and advantages to meet users' needs. Consensus protocols will also continue to evolve, providing new alternatives to enhance network security, efficiency, and decentralization.

Furthermore, decentralized finance (DeFi) is a rapidly expanding area that is expected to experience sustained growth in the years to come. DeFi protocols enable users to access decentralized financial services such as lending, trading, and investments, without relying on traditional intermediaries. DeFi offers an interesting alternative to traditional financial services, providing benefits such as reduced costs, increased accessibility, and greater transparency.

Non-fungible tokens (NFTs) are also a booming area. NFTs allow for the creation and management of unique digital assets, such as artworks, videos, and games. NFTs offer new possibilities for artists, creators, and game developers, allowing them to create and sell unique digital assets in the market.

In terms of use cases, cryptocurrencies have the potential to transform numerous sectors. Financial transactions and money transfers can be simplified and accelerated through the use of cryptocurrencies. Cryptocurrencies can also offer advantages in sectors such as real estate, healthcare, and utilities.

Lastly, cryptocurrency regulation is strengthening in many countries, which should contribute to increased investor confidence and cryptocurrency adoption. However, regulation needs to strike a balance to avoid stifling innovation and market growth.

Acknowledgments

First and foremost, I would like to express my sincere gratitude to all the readers who have taken the time to delve into the fascinating world of cryptocurrencies through this book. It is thanks to you that this work takes on its true meaning. Your curiosity and interest in the subject are the essence of this book, and I hope it has helped you gain a better understanding of the challenges and opportunities associated with the cryptocurrency revolution.

I would also like to thank all the experts, researchers, and enthusiasts in the field of cryptocurrencies, without whom this book would not have been possible. Their hard work and discoveries have not only shaped the industry but also helped make this subject accessible and engaging for everyone. I have studied and compared numerous sources to support the arguments presented in this book, aiming to provide you with a clear and accurate vision of this ever-evolving ecosystem.

As you journeyed through the pages of this book, I have tried to take you on a voyage through the world of cryptocurrencies, offering you an enriching and exciting reading experience.

This book represents the culmination of my passion for cryptocurrencies and my desire to share this knowledge with you. I hope that through these pages, you have felt this passion and that it has inspired you to further deepen your knowledge on the subject.

Cryptocurrencies are a revolution that is rapidly transforming our world, and it is essential to understand the associated challenges and opportunities.

In conclusion, I encourage you to continue exploring the world of cryptocurrencies and closely follow the innovations and developments that shape it. This book is just the beginning of your journey into this exciting universe, and I hope it has provided you with the keys to become a true expert in the field.

Once again, thank you for reading and for your interest. May your journey in the world of cryptocurrencies be filled with discoveries and opportunities!

Sincerely,